Women in Decentralized Rural Governance

Women in Decentralized Rural Governance

Dr. Kamal Kumar Srivastava

KALPAZ

First Published, 2020

Published by

Kalpaz Publications
C-30, Satyawati Nagar,
Delhi – 110052
Ph.: 011-47034999, 9811692060
www.kalpazpublications.com
E-mail: kalpaz@hotmail.com

Printed at: G. Print Process, Delhi

Cataloging in Publication Data—DK
Courtesy: D.K. Agencies (P) Ltd. <docinfo@dkagencies.com>

Srivastava, Kamal Kumar, author.
Women in decentralized rural governance / by Dr. Kamal Kumar Srivastava.
pages cm
Includes bibliographical references.
ISBN 9789353241926

1. Women—Political activity—India. 2. Rural women—Political activity—India. 3. Panchayat—India. 4. Women in rural development—India. 5. Decentralization in government—India. I. Title.

LCC HQ1236.5.I4S65 2019 | DDC 305.420954 23

Contents

Dedicated to

My better half
Dr. Arun Lata Srivastava

Preface and Acknowledgement

Indian polity has been striving for establishing democratic goals through modernizing its political and administrative institutions. With a change in development paradigms, the focus of development planning has shifted to participatory development with social justice and equity. It called for decentralized administration, ensuring people's participation in decision making and giving priorities to their local needs. The 73rd Constitutional Amendment Act 1992 made the provision for ensuring local self governance through empowering local governments. Thus, the units of the Local Self-Governments were given statutory status with establishing of Panchayats at three tiers. Importantly, the local bodies have become the units of the government to have a share in decision making and active participation in development process for socio-economic development of the region. With the enactment of State Conformity Amendment Act 1994, the process of functional and financial devolution to the local bodies was initiated by the State Governments. Political participation of women has gained momentum in India as gender mainstreaming in political institutions has been supported by political activists.Women's share in local governments has no doubt has increased significantly due to the process of decentralization and reservation provided to them. However, their share in higher level political institutions and decision making bodies is still low.

Present study intends to focus upon various aspects of women's functioning in the gram panchayats and its impact on overall rural development. Investigation into these institutions throws light on the actual role played by the women especially at the third strata of governance in solving local problems. The study makes an attempt to examine to what extent affirmative action has helped women to get politically empowered. It attempts to explore the extent to which the Act has succeeded in pursuing the agenda of equal rights for women and concern for recognition of women as equal partner in local administration. The study covers very significant areas of woman heads' life specially the dimensions of change in their social and economic life. The study has been divided into seven chapters. Chapter 1st is introductory which provides rationale, objectives and research methodology. Chapter 2nd deals with review of literature. Chapter 3rd is political empowerment of women and their representation in political institutions in India. . Chapter 4th deals with profile of women Sarpanches. Chapter 5th is related with analysis of role and responsibilities of women sarpanches in rural development and governance. Chapter 6th examines problems and challenges of women sarpanches. Chapter 7th is concluding one, which highlights the main research findings and remedies.

Inspiration encouragement, assistance, cooperation and support from professors, friends, colleagues and above all my family have been vital for accomplishment of any task of life. It is also true in case of present work, for which I have deep sense of gratitude to my professors, friends, colleagues and development professionals. I am highly grateful to ICSSR, New Delhi for entrusting the study to me and providing financial support for perusing the study. I would like to place on record my heartfelt gratitude for the continued support as well as cooperation to Faculty of Department of Public Administration, Lucknow University, Lucknow. I place on record the sincere appreciation of Prof. S. N Singh, Director, Institute of applied Research and Development, Lucknow for encouragement and allowing the use of infrastructure for smooth conduct of study. I am thankful to Dr. S. S. Chauhan, Department of Public Administration, Lucknow University for extending all kind of support in smooth conduct of study. We are thankful to Dr. Rajesh Modi, Principal, Petlad College of Commerce, Anand, Gujarat for his support in smooth conduct of field survey. We place on record the sincere appreciation of Prof. S. C. Arora, Former Head, Department of Public Administration, M. D. University, Rohtak, Haryana for extending support in field survey in Haryana.

I am thankful to Dr. A.K. Singh, Assistant Director, Regional Centre for Urban and Environmental Studies, Lucknow University, Lucknow for taking pains and going through the report and suggesting valuable modifications for enrichment of the quality of research. I place on record sincere appreciation of my better half Dr. Arun Lata Srivastava for constant inspiration and support during the conduct of study. I am thankful to Ms. Gayatri Singh for assisting me in data entry in computer through use of SPSS and tabulation. Lastly I am thankful to Mr. Sunil Barar for giving the manuscript a shape within record time.

Dr. Kamal Kumar Srivastava

Chapter - 1

Introduction

As we approach 21st Century Indian polity has been striving for establishing democratic goals through modernizing its political and administrative institutions. With a change in development paradigms, the focus of development planning has shifted to participatory development with social justice and equity. It called for decentralized administration, ensuring people's participation in decision making and giving priorities to their local needs. The 73rd and 74th Constitutional Amendment Acts 1992 made the provision for ensuring local self governance through empowering local bodies. Thus, the units of the Local Self-Government were given statutory status and state governments were given the mandatory provisions for establishing Panchayats at three tiers. Importantly, the local bodies have become the units of the government to have a share in decision making and active participation in development process for socio-economic development of the region. Though, the provision of local bodies particularly, Panchayats may be traced out in the historical text, monuments and excavation sites. The role of Panchayats in development has been found praiseworthy in ancient period; however, the credit for strengthening of Panchayats in modern period goes to Bruisers. Due to lack of financial and functional autonomy, the Panchayats could not perform well, and because of non-statutory status of Panchayats, State Governments had no mandatory powers to establish the units of Local Self Government. With the enactment of State Conformity Amendment Act 1994, the process of functional and financial devolution to the local bodies was initiated by the State Governments.

State local fiscal relations in the context of 73rd and 74th Amendment Acts have acquired a new meaning and significance. The inadequacy of finances has been a major impediment in the effective functioning of local bodies in India. Their financial position is being revamped through the mechanism of State Finance Commissions. The existing sources of

Panchayats at all levels are highly inadequate to meet out their fiscal needs. Therefore, the task of State Finance Commissions has become more difficult and challenging one. Though, functions and finances have been devolved to local bodies but there is mismatch between them. Even though, funds have been transferred by Union Finance Commissions and State Finance Commissions to local bodies, these bodies face fiscal deficit and there are serious challenges to sustain and maintain core services and to fulfill the committed liabilities by the Panchayats. Therefore, there is an urgent need to assess the potential of Panchayat finances and suggesting policy measures for augmenting their resources.

Political participation of women has gained momentum in India as gender mainstreaming in political institutions has been supported by political activists. The role of women in freedom struggle and feminist movement has been significant however; their representation in political institutions and decision making process is still to be low. Their representation in Parliament and state legislatures is reported less than 10 per cent which is much low as compared to the most of the Muslim countries. Women's share in local governments has no doubt has increased significantly due to the process of decentralization and reservation provided to them. However, their share in higher level political institutions and decision making bodies is still low. The recent debate for the reservation of seats for women in legislative bodies has no doubt created political conscious among the political activists for providing increased opportunities for women in political institutions and decision making bodies. However, most of the political parties and leaders are still in doldrums for providing quota to women for their political empowerment. Though women representation in local governments has significantly increased in post 73rd and 74th Amendment Acts , however, their political participation is still low . The proposed study will be helpful in understanding the dynamics of political participation of women, background characteristics of elected women representatives in local governments, their participation in governance and suggest road map for enhancing the political empowerment of women.

Decentralization and Panchayati Raj

Decentralization has become a buzz word today. Numerous definitions of decentralization emerge from the literature (Davis, et.al., 1994). The term refers to changes which occur within political systems. This, rules out three of six things which are sometimes discussed. The first type of change to be excluded is sometimes called decentralization by default. This happens when government institutions become so ineffective that they fail almost entirely to make the influence of central authorities penetrate down to lower level arenas, and people at the gross roots become heartily cynical about government. When this occurs in countries, voluntary organizations or NGO's, take part in development projects and share resources with government. The second thing to be excluded is privatization, the handover of task formerly performed by state agencies to the private sector (World Bank, 1995). Privatization often involves a shift of power and resources from one major, centralized power centre to another. We also set aside one further type of decentralization, namely, delegation of some responsibilities for development programmes or projects to parastatal agencies. This leaves us with three key definitions: (i) decentralization or administrative decentralization; (ii) fiscal decentralization; (iii) devolution or democratic decentralization. Decentralization refers to the dispersal of agents of higher levels of government into lower level arenas (Rondinelli, 1981, and Parker, 1995). It may be described as administrative decentralization. Second, the term decentralization some times refers to downward fiscal transfers, by which higher levels in a system code influence over budgets and financial decisions to lower levels. This authority may pass to decentralized bureaucrats who are accountable only to superior at higher levels, or to unelected appointees selected from higher level. Finally there is devolution - the transfer of resources and power (and often tasks) to lower level authorities which are largely or wholly independent of higher levels of government, and which are democratic in some way and to some degree. It is recognized that decentralization of resources and responsibilities without (democratizing) political reforms would have been incomplete and probably, not conducive to society effective results (World Bank, 1995).

Democratic decentralization can take varied forms. It clearly includes cases in which the persons in authority within institutions at intermediate and or local levels are elected by secret ballots. Elections may be direct or indirect. The persons who are elected may be the members of a council, or the executive head of an authority, or both. Elections are usually on a first-past-the-post basis, but they some times make use of some form of proportional representation. Decentralization can entail transfers of power to different levels within political systems. It can be bestowed on one or more intermediate levels. When it involves the creation of fully blown governments at the regional level, it qualifies as federalism. But more limited powers may go to intermediate levels, in experiments which fall short of outright federal restructuring.

The causes of decentralization differ substantially from one place to another. The multiplicity of theories and the diversity of experiences suggest the possible validity of the following propositions (Huntington, 1992):

- No single factor is sufficient to explain decisions to decentralize in all countries or in a single country.
- No single factors are necessary to decisions or decentralize in all countries.
- Decentralization in each country is the result of a combination of causes.
- The combination of causes producing decentralization varies from country to country.

The degeneration of patronage systems and the ruling parties in less developed countries played a role. The regimes faced mounting demands from organized interests, yet sluggish economic growth and increasing corruption by political activities at all level, undermined their ability to respond to those demands. The oil shocks of the mid and late 1970's compounded that problem and caused others. Many national leaders over centralized power in the interests of personal rule and that undermined the autonomy resources, effectiveness and responsiveness of ruling parties and formal institutions. By 1970's, it was becoming increasingly possible for small enterprises in many sectors to compete with larger companies-including state owned enterprises. This was partly result of technological innovations. This impelled all manner of decision makers towards greater decentralization. The two paradigms which had long dominated political analyses of less developed countries and the political development/ modernization school and dependency theory become increasingly less convincing during the 1980's. New modes of analysis gained popularity in their place and helped to prepare the ground for experiments with decentralization (Manor, 1997). During the 1980's some donor agencies also began to shift their emphasis away from large scale development programmes to more modest, micro level projects into which grass roots communities could be drawn as participants, in the hope of making development more sustainable. This helped open the way to decentralization. The collapses of the Soviet System and the end of the cold war have also played a role. It lead to the globalization and restructuring of society, economy and polity. The influence of Gandhian ideas in India has always ensured a some what wider constituency for decentralization than in most other countries. But the lack of enthusiasm for such views in Nehru's circle and among India's constitution makers ensured that the elected councils which were created during the 1950's at local and intermediate levels had only very limited powers. Thereafter, national leaders' preoccupations with large scale development projects and state level politician's aversion to sharing power with elected members of lower level councils largely thwarted decentralization. Decentralization assists in tackling the low collective action potential of small farmers and of other, even poorer groups. It has genuine promise in fostering, over time, a more equitable balance of power both between local communications and higher levels of government, and between more and less prosperous groups within local arenas (Manor, 1997). Decentralization strengthens civil society. It integrates pre-existing, informal arrangements and processes at the local level for managing resources and local affairs into the official political process. This can enhance the sustainability of development programmes and policies. Decentralization makes rural dwellers more aware of government policies, and better able to differentiate between those which are beneficial and those which are not (Crook and Manor, 1994). Decentralization now helps ordinary people to develop their analytical capacities and to make use of them. Decentralization promotes the flow of information from people at lower level to the upper reaches of government. Thus it enables government to become more responsive. It increases hugely the numbers of people at lower level in political systems who know how much public money is available for development. This promotes political stability. Decentralization can enhance political stability more responsive to people at lower levels, it can break down popular cynicism about politics and increase the legitimacy of political system. Second, by creating a large number of elected posts in authorities at lower levels, it generates opportunities for political activities at those levels who aspire to a role in government. This eases their frustrations which can threaten stability. Third, it eases the frustrations of opposition parties by increasing the number of arenas in which there are political prizes to be won. After decentralization, elections occur not just to the national presidency or legislature, but to authorities at regional and local levels. This helps to persuade opposition parties and interests, whose candidates lose elections for one of those bodies, to remain engaged with the democratic process, since they may win in another arena at the next opportunity (Jenkins, 1997).

The imperatives of decentralized planning in India have been repeatedly emphasized in the Five Year Plan documents in our country. However, the progress in this direction remained slow and faltering despite frequent changes in the policy prescriptions. Indian economy has reached a stage in the process of development wherein the existence and survival of democratic politicization calls for immediate implementation of the process of decentralized planning. The structural, technological, institutional and organizational impediments to development can be effectively dealt only when the process of planning is approached and viewed in the proximity of the specific areas and the local public.

The 73rd and 74th Constitutional Amendment Acts, 1992 made the provision for ensuring local self governance through empowering local bodies. Thus, the units of the local self governments were given statutory status and state governments were given the mandatory provisions for establishing three tiers of local governments both in rural and urban areas. Importantly, the local bodies have become the units of the governments to have a share in decision making and active participation in development process for social-economic development of the region. The constitution of 74th Amendment Act, 1992, has marked the beginning of a historical reform to decentralize power at the grass root level in urban areas of the country. This act has provided a constitutional form to the structure and mandate of municipalities to enable them to function as an effective democratic institution of local self government. One of its important objectives is to promote people's participation in planning, provision and delivery of civic services. It introduced some fundamental changes in the system of municipal governance with a new structure, additional devolution of functions, planning responsibilities, new system of fiscal transfers and empowerment of women and the weaker sections of the society (Agrawal, 2005). There have been significant changes in the institutional structure for the financing and management of basic services in the post decentralization period. Prior to 1994, the central government was not involved in any transfer of resources to the ULB's.

The world wide trend towards decentralization has attracted the attention of policy makers and has led to the discussion about its benefits and costs. Most of the countries have placed the strengthening of local governments or decentralization on development policy agenda. However, the share of expenditures made by sub national governments has not increased in the last two decades. Perhaps the economic conditions have not suited the adoption of comprehensive decentralization schemes. However, decentralization as a panacea for many of the ill afflicting society, defects of development models and social problems has been recognized by policy makers. It is perceived as a means to improve delivery of public goods, services, people's active participation in development process, and governance as well as increased resources mobilization. The impact of decentralization on efficiency, growth and corruption is likely to be positive. The complex phenomenon of decentralization may be classified into three types, de-concentration, delegation, and devolution. In de-concentration, the decision making power is with higher level government, and the lower level is merely employed to implement the higher level's policies and programmes. In delegation, the higher level government delegation decision making power to the lower level for specified functions. Only in devolution is decision making power shared between the higher level and lower levels of government so that genuine decentralization is apparent. Again, administrative decentralization is necessary to implement political decisions while fiscal decentralization is required for improving in the efficiency in the delivery of public services and ensuring accountability and transparency in governance (Singh et.al., 2005).

Decentralization to rural and urban governments began even before independence. Despite Gandhiji's commitment to village governments, the first draft of Constitution did not make any provisions for Panchayats. When the provisions were made, they were confined to non-justiciable parts of the Constitution. In 1957, the Balwantroy Mehta Committee recommended democratic decentralization by setting up Panchayati Raj Institutions, and devolving the necessary resources, powers and authority to them. However, the committee did not make provisions for fiscal decentralization, the K. Santhanan Committee ws set up in 1963 to look into finances of Panchayats. The Committee recommended the powers to levy a special tax on land revenue and homes, consolidation of all grants of the state level and devolution to PRI's and the establishment of a Panchayati Raj Finance Corporation to look into the financial resources of PRI's and provide loans and financial assistance to grassroots level governments. Ashok Mehta Committee, in 1978, for the first time recommended including Panchayats in the Constitution. However, the thrust shifted from the Panchayat as a development organization to the Panchayat as a political institution. Again, L.M. Singhvi Committee in 1986 recommended the Constitutional recognition of local self government and the non-inclusion of political parties in Panchayat elections. In September, 1991, the Congress government introduced the 72nd (Panchayats) and 73rd (Nagar Palika) Constitutional Amendment Bills and finally, on April 24, 1993, the Constitutional Amendment formally came into force after ratification by more than half of the state assemblies. When both houses of Parliament passed the bills, the sequence of the bills changed to the 73rd and 74th Amendment, respectively. The feature of 73rd Amendment include: (i) granting PRI's constitutional status; (ii) empowering socially and economically disadvantaged groups such as SC's, ST's, women; (iii) ensuring free, fair and regular elections; (iv) identifying a list of subjects to come under the jurisdiction of PRI's; (v) uniform three tier PRI structure with village, block and district levels; (vi) direct election to all seats for all members at all levels; (vii) uniform five year term for Panchayats; (viii) twenty-nine subjects eligible for devolution to Panchayats; (ix) setting of State Finance

Commission once in five years to review PRI financial position and make suitable recommendations for fund distribution to Panchayats. The Constitutional Amendment, however, excluded the Scheduled Areas, except for reservation to Scheduled Tribes. Bhuria Committee, in 1994, extended the provisions to Scheduled Areas and suggested modification to strengthen institutions of local self government, the Provisions for Extension to Scheduled Areas (PESA) came into effect in 1996 (Singh et.al., 2005).

Thus, the states and union territories amended their respective Panchayat Acts. These amended acts provided for uniformity in terms of three tier local government's at the district, block and village levels: Zilla Panchayats, Panchayat Samitis, and Gram Panchayats. Almost all the states have transferred subjects to panchayats in varying degrees, and several have transferred all 29 subjects. However, the nominal transfer of subjects is not enough to enable Panchayats to perform these functions.

The Constitutional Amendment provided for the creation of State Finance Commissions (SRC's) to review and make recommendations on Panchayats finances. Most states constituted SFC's, which have common terms of reference. The SFC's are required to recommend financial support from the state, and the principles for the determination of taxes, tolls, and fees that can be assigned to or appropriated by the local bodies. SFC's in different states followed different ways of determining the resource requirement of local bodies. But in absence of clear expenditure assignments, all SFC's encountered problems in such assessment. They also faced problems of relevant data. Thus, different SFC's devised different methods for devolution of plan funds to local bodies. These methods depended heavily on population, area and development level.

Status of Democratic Decentralization

Democratic decentralization and involvement of people in decision-making process recognized by the Constituent Assembly which enshrined it in the Constitution as one of the Directive Principles of the State Policy. Several initiatives were taken in the 1950s and 1960s to promote democratic decentralization. However, the 73rd and 74th Constitutional Amendment Acts mark a watershed in the history of governance in the country. Panchayati Raj Institutions (PRIs) were introduced as a distinct third tier of government. At the time of the formulation of the Ninth Five Year Plan, the 73rd & 74th Amendment Acts were in the process of being operationalized. It was expected that PRIs that come up under the new Acts would be devolved functions, finances and the functionaries to enable them to emerge as institutions of self-government.

The provisions of the 73rd Amendment Act were extended to the Schedule V areas of nine states i.e. Andhra Pradesh, Chhattisgarh, Gujarat, Himachal Pradesh, Jharkhand, Madhya Pradesh, Maharashtra, Orissa and Rajasthan under Central Act 40 of 1996 i.e. The Provisions of the Panchayats (Extension to the Scheduled Areas) Act, 1996. The Act is intended to enable tribal communities to assume control over their own destiny to preserve and conserve their traditional rights over natural resources. All States barring Jharkhand have enacted State Legislation to give effect to the provisions contained in Act 40, 1996. States other than Jharkhand have also amended most of the subject laws to bring them in conformity with the provisions of the Central Act, 40. The basic features of 73rd Constitutional Amendment are shown in Box 1.1.

Box: 1.1

73rd Constitutional Amendment: Basic Features

- Constitutional status to the panchayats and gives it uniformity by making the three-tier system a permanent feature.
- Panchayats to be constituted in every State at the village, intermediate and district level, except States with a population not exceeding 20 lakh.
- Establishing a Gram Sabha in each village, exercising powers and performing functions at the village level, as the State may provide by law.
- Members of panchayats at all levels will be elected through direct elections. The election of the chairperson at the intermediate and district level will be through indirect elections.
- Seats are reserved for SCs and STs at all levels according to their population. Not less than one-third of seats are reserved for women.
- The office of Chairperson will also be subject to this provision.
- A uniform five-year term has been granted to the panchayats. In case of dissolution, elections should be held within six months of the date of dissolution.
- Panchayats are entrusted with (i) preparing plans and implementing schemes for social justice and economic development; (ii) in regard to matters listed in the 11th Schedule.
- State legislature authorities the panchayats to levy, collect and appropriate suitable local taxes. The Government can make grant-in-aid to the panchayats from the Consolidated Fund of the concerned State.
- Review of the financial position of the panchayats will be undertaken by a finance commission, which shall be constituted every five years.

Source: 73rd Constitution Amendment, 1992.

Eleventh Schedule was added in the Indian Constitution which provides a basis for functioning and devolution of powers to the Panchayati Raj Institutions in India. The features of the Eleventh Schedule are shown in Box 1.2.

Box: 1.2

"Eleventh Schedule" (Article 243G)

- Agriculture, including agricultural extension
- Land improvement, implementation of land reforms, land consolidation and soil conservation
- Minor irrigation, water management and watershed development
- Animal husbandry, dairying and poultry
- Fisheries
- Social forestry and farm forestry
- Minor forest produce
- Small scale industries, including food processing industries
- Khadi, village and cottage industries
- Rural housing
- Drinking water
- Fuel and fodder
- Roads, culverts, bridges, ferries, waterways and other means of communication.
- Rural electrification, including distribution of electricity
- Non-conventional energy sources
- Poverty alleviation programmes
- Education, including primary and secondary schools
- Technical training and vocational education
- Adult and non-formal education
- Libraries
- Cultural activities
- Markets and fairs
- Health and sanitation, including hospitals, primary health centres and dispensaries
- Family welfare
- Women and child development
- Social welfare, including welfare of the handicapped and mentally retarded
- Welfare of the weaker sections, and in particular, of the Scheduled Castes and the Scheduled Tribes
- Public distribution system
- Maintenance of community assets

Source: 73rd Constitution Amendment, 1992.

Democratic decentralization in the Indian context is not an end itself. It is a process for harnessing, channelizing and realizing the energies of the people with a view to bringing about social transformation where every member of the society gains his or her rightful place in the social, economic and political life of the country. PRIs are expected to play a multifaceted role. They are vehicles for political education and training in leadership. They have to be responsive to the needs of the community, impart values of equality and liberty, be transparent, accountable and efficient and to provide opportunities for mass participation in the process of development (Kanshi, K., 2005). On the eve of the formulation of the Tenth Five Year Plan, the country has the experience of 7-8 years in the functioning of the PRIs. Elections in many states have taken place for the second time. In the terminal year of the Ninth Plan, it was felt that the time was opportune to review the progress of democratic decentralization in the country and suggest measures for further deepening of this process in the Tenth Five Year Plan so that PRIs could play their designated role in the socio-economic development of the country.

Statement of Research Problem

Women empowerment has been an ongoing debate in India and elsewhere. Indian women occupying a subordinate position to men need to be empowered to overcome social, political and economic discrimination. There were several attempts to improve the position of women after India got independence. The 73rd Amendment Act is a major step towards political empowerment of women through Panchayati Raj Institutions. This has resulted in the entry of large number of women into decision making bodies in the rural areas, who were otherwise home makers. On the other hand, participation of women in Panchayati Raj Institutions had lead to lot of debate on the functioning of women members in these institutions. Contradictory reports about the story of women member's participation, some triumphant, other tragic has enhanced the curiosity of researchers.

The term political participation generally refers to those voluntary activities of members of a society, in the selection of rulers and formation of public policy. Since popular sovereignty is one of the inseparable attributes of democracy, the right to participate is an important aspect of democratic government and an inherent right in a democratic process. Political participation is a basic ingredient of every political system. Participation helps the individual to be effective and associates him with the political system. Higher the rate and levels, the more varied the forms of political participation. It is vital to the proper functioning of a democratic polity. The International Encyclopedia of Social Sciences defined political participation as the principal means by which consent is granted or withdrawn in a democracy and rulers are made accountable to the ruled (International Encyclopedia, 1968). It signifies such proceedings like voting, seeking information, discussing and proselytizing, attending meetings, contributing financially and communicating with representatives (International Encyclopedia, 1968).

Many writers have rightly argued that political participation of citizens is the distinguishing mark of modern states. More than anything else, the modem state is distinguished from the traditional ones by the extent to which people participate in politics (Das, 1997). High levels of political participation are usually associated with democracy, which is beneficial both to the individual and to the society. Political participation has been considered as a 'sine qua non' of democracy (Das, 1997). Political participation has been characterized as a civic duty, as a sign of political health and the best method of ensuring that one's private interests are not neglected. Although political power in every society is monopolized by a few, the incumbents of political authority in every system are found to be quite keen on ensuring some amount of political participation by the people. Thus, by involving the many in the matters of the state, political participation fosters stability and order by reinforcing the legitimacy of political authority.

Political participation is a term that has many meanings. The term is applied to the activities of people from all levels of political system. Sometimes the term is applied more to political orientations than to activities. Political participation is defined in such a way as to include the exercise of power in nongovernmental as well as government spheres. It is true that there exists a great deal of confusion with regard to what is meant by that term; "Participation may be viewed from two angles again-intensity and width. How deeply a person is involved in an issue and to what extent he would go towards achievement of this objective would determine the intensity. Width arises because of the complex nature of political activity that requires participation in different issues ranging from casting votes to participating in a technical expert committee or becoming a minister" (Sheshadri, 1976).

Political participation may be defined as those actions of private citizens by which they seek to influence or support government and politics (Milbrath & Goel, 197). This definition is broader than most others, as it includes not only active roles that people pursue in order to influence political outcomes but also ceremonial and support activities. To Almond and Powel, "political participation is the involvement of the members of the society in the decision making process of the system" (Almond & Powelll, 1975). Mc Closky defines, "political participation implies those voluntary activities by which members of a society share in the selection of rulers and directly or indirectly, in the formulation of public policy" (Dowse, 1972). Verba and Pye define it as, "Those activities by private citizens that are more or less directly aimed at influencing the selection of governmental personnel and the actions they take" (Verba & Nie, 1972). Political participation of elected women representatives will be measured in terms of voting, nominations for political posts in parties , pressure groups, election fray , holding positions in political and administrative bodies or institutions, decision making process, attending meetings, raising issues and concern for development and governance.

Present study intends to focus upon various aspects of women's functioning in the gram panchayats and its impact on overall development of women. Investigation into these institutions throws light on the actual role played by the women especially at the third strata of governance in solving local problems. The study makes an attempt examine to what extent affirmative action has helped women to get politically empowered. It attempts to explore the extent to which the Act has succeeded in pursuing the agenda of equal rights for women and concern for recognition of women as equal partner in local administration. It examines the various dimensions of political empowerment of women through gram panchayats on the basis of empirical investigations in the Udupi district of Karnataka state in India. In fact this study is an attempt to find out whether 'Udupi Model of Women's Political Empowerment' can be construed or is it emerging in this particular district through the analysis of political participation in the Panchayati Raj Institutions. The study covers very significant areas of woman heads' life specially the dimensions of change in their social and economic life.

Rationale of the Study

Women's political participation has been considered a major measure of women's empowerment. Globally, through histories of the world we have records of very few regents, sovereigns, and active agents in nobility who were women .Gender equality and gender equity are emerging as major challenges in the recent times. As Nobel Prize winner Amartya Sen has pointed out, "Democracy is not the goal of development; it is the primary means of development." Women's participation in political processes is important for strengthening democracy and for their struggle against marginalization, trivialization and oppression. Coming up of women as a strong group would change the prevailing political practices, the nature and content of debate in the legislature and women's issues can be taken care of from the feminists' perspective both in policy formulation and implementation. Women are considered extremely pivotal in the process of change in the rural areas. Women's participation in Panchayats has provided them opportunities in the decision making process. It has proved to be the most effective instrument in bringing about change in their way of life in terms of economic well being and adoption of new technology. Their entry into Panchayati Raj Institutions, both as members as well as heads of Panchayats, has pushed them into the policy making and implementation process in a big way. A few states have already introduced 50 percent reservation to women in local governments. Women are also coming forward in the local politics and their participation in the decision making and governance of development programmes and schemes is gradually increasing, however, they face problems and challenges in performance of their responsibilities and roles. Their problems are manifold which include proxy attendance in meetings, role conflicts as they face grievances of family, society and governments, social barriers, male dominance in decision making, lack of knowledge, information and educational backwardness, etc. Thus, it is imperative to study the opportunities and challenges of elected women heads of PRIs in Haryana.

Objectives of the Study

The aim of the study is to understand the extent of empowerment achieved by women heads of Panchayati Raj Institutions in Haryana and Gujarat The study aims at a descriptive study of the status of the woman heads of Village Panchayats in Haryana and Gujarat. The main objectives of the study are as follows:

- To study the political participation of women in India in general and Haryana and Gujarat in particular,
- To examine the socio-economic conditions of the women heads of village panchayats in Haryana and Gujarat,
- To verify the roles and responsibilities of women heads in Village Panchayats in Haryana and Gujarat,
- To examine the problems and challenges faced by the women heads in Village Panchayats in Haryana and Gujarat,
- To draw policy implications for improving the functioning of the PRIs in India in selected states in particular and also for empowerment of women.

Hypotheses of the Study

The status of the women in Haryana is not uniform among all the different communities. Factors like patriarchal family, marriage and divorce, degree of acculturation and urbanization, level of education and so on many have contributed to this variations. The status of women in this region varies along with the differences in the level of socio-economic development.

The study has been conducted keeping in view of the following hypotheses

- Women participation in political institutions especially PRIs have increased since enactment of 73rd Constitutional Amendment.
- Women are facing problems in performance of their roles and responsibilities in the male dominated society and political set up.
- There has been positive change in the political landscape due to reservation of women in local governments.
- Most of Sarpanches are less educated with very poor understanding and knowledge of the gram panchayat manuals, their rights and responsibilities, poverty alleviation and employment generating schemes which are currently operational in the rural areas
- Political participation of women in the local rural bodies has hardly made any noticeable dent in terms of raising their social and economic status, improving the literacy ratio, providing health, maternity and sanitation benefits to women and ameliorating violence, oppression, menace of dowry, rape, discrimination etc.

Operational Definitions

- **Empowerment:** Empowerment refers to improvement of living conditions and facilitation of socio-economic development of an individual. It is about one's overall developments that increase his/her ability to realize his/her own preference in life.
- **PRIs:** PRIs refer to local government constituted as per 73rd Constitution Amendment Act in 1992. These institutions are Village Panchayat, Panchayat Samiti and Zila Parishad of Haryana State.

Research Design

The descriptive research design has been adopted in this study. The study critically analyzed the socio-economic and political conditions of woman heads of PRIs of Haryana. The study also focused upon the roles and responsibilities of women heads. The researcher also examined the problems and challenges faced by the women heads in Panchayati Raj Institutions in Haryana and Gujarat. We have also made an attempt to understand the level of empowerment on the basis of autonomy in the family, mobility within and outside the community and decision making powers among the women heads. The study also draws policy implications for improving the functioning of the PRIs in India and Haryana and Gujarat in particular and also for empowerment of women.

Universe of the Study

The universe of the present study is the elected women heads of Village Panchayats in the State of Haryana and Gujarat.

Sampling of the Study

In the present study sample and census methods is used to select the respondents. A multi stage stratified random sampling method was applied for the selection of the sample of women Sarpaches for the study. At the first stage four districts i.e. Jhajjar, Kurukshetra Hisar and Gurgaon of Haryana were selected randomly. In the state of Gujarat, Ahmadabad, Mehsana, Sabarkantha and Anand were selected for field survey. At the second stage, all the women sarpanches of each district were taken as respondents. Overall, 596 women Sarpanches were randomly selected for field survey.

Sources of Data

The study has conducted on the basis of two sources of data. The first one is primary data collection and the second one is Secondary data collection..

(A) Primary Sources

The primary source of data was the 596 units i.e. women heads of Gram Panchayats in the State of Haryana and Gujarat. The primary data were collected through face to face interview with the respondents and also by observation.

(B) Secondary Sources

The researcher has collected relevant information from reliable sources from government department i.e. Department of Panchayati Raj, Government of India.

Tools for Data Collection

In order to fulfill the objectives of the study the researcher used both the quantitative and qualitative methods during data collection. The following tools were used for data collection.

(i) Interview Schedule

A well structured interview schedule was prepared for data collection. The interview schedule was divided into three parts. The first part includes the socio, cultural and economic profile of respondents and their political participation, second part of the schedule includes women's role and responsibilities in PRIs and the last part includes their perception pertaining to decentralized governance and role conflicts, etc. Both closed ended and open ended questions were given in the interview schedule. The open ended questions gave the respondents the freedom to record their own experiences as Heads of Panchayati Raj Institutions.

(ii) Observation

Apart from interview schedule observation method is also applied to supplement the information supplied by the respondents during the filling up of schedules. Observation method was used to collect the necessary information regarding their socio-cultural and political practices. The researcher has made a number of visits to the Heads of all the tier of PRIs and gathered information.

The field survey was conducted with the help of structured interview schedules. The researcher pre tested the interview schedule on women Sarpanches. After pre-tested the interview schedule the researcher made some modification in this schedule. The researcher made some changes on the structure of the questionnaire like modification in open ended questions to close ended questions specifically related to the roles and responsibilities of the women heads.

Analysis and Interpretation of the Data

The filled interview schedules were thoroughly checked, edited and processed through SPSS for the purpose of analysis. Univariate and bivariate tables were prepared to find out the relationship between the variables. Inferences, results and conclusions were drawn out from the analysis of data. The policy recommendations also made on the basis of analysis of research findings and critical appreciation of pertinent literature.

Limitations of the Study

The present study has its own limitations. All the limitations are as follows:

- The study is confined to the women Heads of Village Panchayats only.
- The findings of the study are based on the responses received from the respondents.
- The area of the study is limited to the State of Haryana and Gujarat.
- The result of the study is based on the primary field work.

Chapter - 2

Review of Literature

A number of studies related to political participation of women has been conducted which depict various dimensions and aspects of political empowerment of women. The conceptualization of political participation has been undergoing drastic changes. Such changes will have a direct impact upon different modes of political participation. Citizens can participate in different and alternative ways to influence the government and the political system. Until recently most survey studies of political participation confined their enquiry to a relatively limited set of political acts. Most of them asked whether a person had voted or not and some went on to ask about such behaviour as attendance at political meetings or rallies, working for a party, making a monetary contribution or seeking a public office (Milbrath & Goel, 1977). However, these alternative ways of political participation depend on the types of citizens who participate, tile way in which they act, the amount of pressure they can to exert and the system's response towards their activities. Thus political participation is more than the vote and more than an activity in the electoral system. Verba and Nie grouped into four broad modes of participation the alternative activities by which citizens can participate in politics, i.e., voting, campaign activity, co-operative activity and citizen-initiated contact (Verba & Nie, 1972). Milbrath and Goel add protest and communication to these modes mentioned by Verba and Nie, which relate individuals to the polity. They are also of the view that political acts could be hierarchically organised from the least difficult to the most difficult, if a person performed a more difficult act, he was likely to perform those that are less difficult as well (Milbrath & Goel, 1977).

It is useful to' consider political participation in a hierarchical sense, but it should also be born in mind that some levels of participation may be absent in some political systems (Rush & Althoff, 1971). Not all political system have elections or a form of voting, some systems severely restrict or ban public meetings and demonstrations, while others forbid the formation of political parties and other types of political or quasi-political orgnisation, and so on (Rush & Althoff, 1971). Explaining the extent of political participation Michael Rush and Philip Althoff added that apathy, alienation and the use of violence vary clearly and considerably from system to system, but remain quite important factors in any examination of political participation (Rush & Althoff, 1971).

Examining the modes of political participation Schonfeld has mentioned ten types of activities which include (I) running for or holding public or party offices, (2) belonging to a party or other political organization, (3) working in an election, (4) attending political meetings or rallies, (5) making financial contribution to a party or a candidate, (6) contacting a public official, (7) publicly expressing a political opinion to convince others, (8) partaking in political discussion, (9) voting, and (10) exposing oneself to political stimuli (Schonfeld, 1975). Political participation is the mother and politics is the child. The former creates and determines politics and hence is of utmost importance both for the nation and the individual. The politics of the nation is determined therefore, by political participation in all its processes (Bala, 1999).

The socio-economic environment will have a direct impact upon political participation. Socio-economic variables include education, occupation, income, age, caste, religion, sex, family background, residence etc. "Political participation", says Robert Lane, "IS a function of age, sex, education and status (Lane, 1959). Thus generally, participation tends to be higher among better educated, members of higher occupational and income groups, middle aged, dominant ethnic and religious groups, people with political family background, settled residents, urban dwellers and members of voluntary associations (Closky, 1968). However, the correlation between political participation and some of these socio-economic variables may vary from culture to culture in different political contexts and their effect on political participation may not be stable.

Ideology can affect political participation, positively or negatively. Normally, those who have firm faith in democratic ideology positively respond to political participation. On the other hand, persons having contempt for democratic ideology show little inclination for political participation. Political participation is associated with political awareness i.e., actual knowledge of political affairs. A wareness is highly connected with interest. In every society the number of citizens who can be described as 'aware' is extremely small. Awareness affects both the quality and amount of participation (Das, 1997). It is to be noted that the three sets of variables are closely linked and intermingled. A change in any of them, can, therefore, increase or decrease the level of political participation.

Another dimension that has to be taken into account is why some people keep off from all forms of political participation or even if they participate they are ready to play only a minimal role. In other words people who participate in most forms of political activity constitute a minority and often a very small minority. The factors, which inhibit political participation, are psychological and emotional. The non-participants are described as apathetic, cynical, alienated and anemic (Roy, 1999). Apathy is characterized by individuals' passivity or abstention from political activity. It may be defined as lack of interest or concern for persons, situations or phenomena in general or particular (Das, 1997). Apathy leads to the decline of political vitality and vigilance widespread apathy increases the chances of opportunists and unscrupulous people to dominate the policy making process (Das, 1997). Thus it is nothing other than lack of interest in politics.

Morris Rosenberg has suggested three major reasons for political apathy. The first reason is perceived consequence of political activity. Second reason is that the individual may regard political activity as futile. The third reason is that political stimuli is an important factor in encouraging political activity and the absence of such stimuli may contribute to feelings of apathy (Roy, 1999). Cynicism is a feeling that the actions and motives of others are to be regarded with suspicion. Robert Auger and his colleagues define cynicism as being contemptuously distrustful of human nature (Roy, 1999). It is observed that a person, who is extremely cynical may well feel that political participation in any form is futile and thus join the ranks of the totally apathetic (Roy, 1999). Alienation is another form of non- participation with respect to a political system. While cynicism refers to a type of distaste for politics and politicians, alienation denotes actual hostility (Das, 1997). Robert Lane defines political alienation as a "person's sense of estrangement from the politics and government of his society and the tendency to think of the government and politics of the nation as run by others for others according to an unfair set of rules (Roy, 1999). According to Robert Lane anemic refers to "a sense of value loss and lack of direction" (Roy, 1999). It denotes a psychological attitude in which the individual experiences a feeling of ineffectiveness. Thus while apathy means lack of interest and cynicism represents an attitude of distaste or disenchantment, both alienation and anemic imply a feeling of estrangement or divorce from the society (Roy, 1999).

The present study is concerned not with political participation in general, but it is only a micro-level study concerned with political participation of women that too at the grassroots levels of political functioning. Participation of women in Panchayati Raj institutions and urban local governments has been an area of much interest in India. Participation in the local government institutions has been viewed as essential in promoting women's conscious-ness and development at the local level as well as in training them for participation in the wider politics. Democratic thinkers haven general linked liberty to the people by the process of political participation. Participation is maximized in local government because, "local institutions are to liberty what primary schools are to science; they put it within people's reach; they teach people to appreciate its peaceful enjoyment and accustom them to make use of it (de Tocqueville, 1966). Karl Mam stood in favour of mass involvement in the process. To him political participation by the masses is at once a process of education and of building up of a capacity for governing the new society (Sheshadri, 1976). It is a fact that woman herself is an important variable capable of determining the nature and scope of political participation and as a result the whole political system in turn.

The attempt to assess and evaluate the level and extent of political participation of women become very much relevant as to the nature and functioning of the political system as a whole. It is particularly more beneficial to political parties and political leaders due to the natural qualities of women such as honesty, affection and sense of duty. The mobilization of women in large numbers weakened the bondage of tradition and encouraged them to develop a perspective on the wider socio-political problems (Kumar, 2000). It is not an argument for feminism. "Feminism is the political theory and practice that struggles to free all women: women of colour, working class women" (Smith, 1982). Milbrath and Goel observed that it is a tradition in almost all societies that politics is mainly an affair of men and that women should fall in line with them politically. The changes brought by modern industrial societies are eroding this sex difference but the impact of tradition is still visible. Men tend to be more psychologically involved in politics than women (Milbrath & Goel, 1977). Studies on sex differences in the political behaviour usually focus on differences in early childhood socialization. Tedin, et.al, however, give more importance to situational factors in sex related differences in political expressiveness than to socialization or structural factor women are less politically expressive because the environment of the house wife or the menial sort of employment available to most women does not encourage them to take part in politics or give stimulation to collect and discuss politically relevant information. Female situational factors, which lead to less political expressiveness become institutionalized and passed on to future generations through the socialization process, which in turn makes it more difficult for women to overcome situational disadvantages (Teden, et.al. 1977).

In India, there is a continued dominance of the upper class in education, administration and structures of government. The eighty-fourth constitution Amendment Bill meant to provide one-third reservation of seats to women in states and central legislative bodies and the controversies around it mirror the contradictions of Indian society (Raman, 2002). The protagonists of the Bill highlight the traditionally sanctioned exclusion of women from the public sphere as crucial. Undoubtedly, women's suppression, in history, has been very important in maintaining upper-class exclusivity and hegemony. Affirmative action for women would certainly play a role in undermining male and upper-caste dominance. There is also a strong resistance on the part of a considerable number of political leaders to 'encroachments' into what has been a traditionally male preserve. The media has characterized the debate as a battle between 'feminists' and 'casteists' (Raman, 2002). In India, the 73rd and 74th amendments passed in 1992 have been instrumental in ensuring a strong representation of women in local government institutions for women in local government and the provision for one third chair persons to be from among the women but there is no reservation of seats for women either in the State Legislative Assembly nor in parliament at the national level. The demand for reservation in the parliament by women's groups has raised many eyebrows and severe criticism. Many times the bill was taken in parliament but failed. Women activists wanted to get this bill passed before the elections to the state assemblies and parliament to be held by the end of 2008. At least once a year a few members of parliament debate the need to reserve 33 percent of seats for women. The bill comes up when the parliament convenes but soon gets shelved with all the ensuing acrimony (Times of India: 2008).

Political participation of women has gained momentum in India as gender mainstreaming in political institutions has been supported by political activists. The role of women in freedom struggle and feminist movement has been significant however; their representation in political institutions and decision making process is still to be low. Women's share in local governments has no doubt has increased significantly due to the process of decentralization and reservation provided to them. However, their share in higher level political institutions and decision making bodies is still low. The recent debate for the reservation of seats for women in legislative bodies has no doubt created political conscious among the political activists for providing increased opportunities for women in political institutions and decision making bodies. However, most of the political parties and leaders are still in doldrums for providing quota to women for their political empowerment. Though women representation in local governments has significantly increased in post 73rd and 74th Amendment Acts, however, their political participation is still low.

Gender equality and women empowerment are the key terms that defined and determined the direction of diverse discourses on women, nationally and globally. The Beijing conference was the most significant milestone in journey towards ensuring gender equality and enriching pragmatic insights into the issues concerning women empowerment (Singh & Srivastava, 2001). Gender equality is central to realizing the Millennium Development Goals. However, gender discrimination across the life cycle is still prevalent in most of the countries across the globe. In India too, gender discrimination is prevalent in its socio-cultural setup. Gender discrimination is pervasive while the degree and forms of inequality may vary; women and girls are deprived of equal access to resources, opportunities and political power in every region of the world. The oppression of girls and women can include the preference for sons over daughters, limited personnel and professional choices for girls and women, the denial of basic human rights and outright gender based violence (UNICEF, 2007). It is agreed that due to globalization, world income is increasing and every third countries is progressing. But when we consider its impact on women, we find different picture. Scholars give different views regarding the impact of globalization on women. We can categorize them into two broader categories. First school of thought includes those scholars who are agreed that women have benefited from the globalization with the growth of world economy. The second school of thought includes the scholars who are of the view that women are negatively affected by globalization. However, globalization has mixed bag of impacts on women. In some areas, positive impacts of globalization on women are visualized however, in certain areas, the negative impact of globalization on women is observed. The socio-cultural impact of globalization is reported mainly negative however, the positive impact of globalization mainly relates with economic aspects.

Political participation is the hallmark of a democratic setup. Nature, success and effectiveness of democracy largely depend on the extent to which equal, effective and actual participation is provided by the system to all its citizens. As women comprise about half of the population, this section of society requires due attention in the system and a due share in process. Citizens' active participation in political affairs in a democracy is crucial and necessary because it provides legitimacy to the system and also strengthens the democratic fabric (Palmer, 1976). Democracy will fail in its objectives if women citizens lack equal opportunity to participate in the governmental decision-making process. They are to be equal partners in the nation-building and political development. Political democracy requires at least a minimum of people's participation in the decision making process. Citizens' participation in political affairs is important because a situation which results in high participation by members of a group normally has higher potential for democracy (Lipset, 1973). Norman D. Palmer defines political participation as the involvement of citizens in such political activities, which directly or indirectly influence the behaviour and actions of decision-makers (Palmer, 1976). It may be viewed as any "Voluntary action, successful or unsuccessful, organised or unorganised, episodic or continuous, employing legitimate or illegitimate methods, intended to influence the choice of public policies, the administration of public affairs, or the choices of political leaders at any level of government, local or national" (Weiner, 1976). It may be pointed out that all citizens do not participate equally or in the same manner in any political process. The political culture of a society greatly influences the nature of political participation of individuals. The real purpose and impact of participation is to make the citizen not a passive spectator but an agent in politics, to enable him to show his disagreement as much as to endorse what is proposed, as much to scotch Initiatives as to launch them, as much to revise, criticize and block as to push, prod and hasten (Mount, 1974). However, if political participation is to have any concrete meaning, particularly in a democratic setup, people should directly or indirectly take part in the decision-making processes which affect their day to day life. Political participation of women in India is reported to be low at all levels of political and administrative institutions, however, there has been increasing trend in participation of women in local governments , both in PRIs and ULBs . This is because of the fact that one third seats of PRIs and ULBs have been reserved for women.

The term political participation generally refers to those voluntary activities of members of a society, in the selection of rulers and formation of public policy. Since popular sovereignty is one of the inseparable attributes of democracy, the right to participate is an important aspect of democratic government and an inherent right in a democratic process. Political participation is a basic ingredient of every political system. Participation helps the individual to be effective and associates him with the political system. Higher the rate and levels, the more varied the forms of political participation. It is vital to the proper functioning of a democratic polity. The International Encyclopedia of Social Sciences defined political participation as the principal means by which consent is granted or withdrawn in a democracy and rulers are made accountable to the ruled (International Encyclopedia, 1968). It signifies such proceedings like voting, seeking information, discussing and proselytizing, attending meetings, contributing financially and communicating with representatives (International Encyclopedia, 1968).

Many writers have rightly argued that political participation of citizens is the distinguishing mark of modern states. More than anything else, the modem state is distinguished from the traditional ones by the extent to which people participate in politics (Das, 1997). High levels of political participation are usually associated with democracy, which is beneficial both to the individual and to the society. Political participation has been considered as a 'sine qua non' of democracy (Das, 1997). Political participation has been characterized as a civic duty, as a sign of political health and the best method of ensuring that one's private interests are not neglected. Although political power in every society is monopolized by a few, the incumbents of political authority in every system are found to be quite keen on ensuring some amount of political participation by the people. Thus, by involving the many in the matters of the state, political participation fosters stability and order by reinforcing the legitimacy of political authority.

Political participation is a term that has many meanings. The term is applied to the activities of people from all levels of political system. Sometimes the term is applied more to political orientations than to activities. Political participation is defined in such a way as to include the exercise of power in nongovernmental as well as government spheres. It is true that there exists a great deal of confusion with regard to what is meant by that term; "Participation may be viewed from two angles again-intensity and width. How deeply a person is involved in an issue and to what extent he would go towards achievement of this objective would determine the intensity. Width arises because of the complex nature of political activity that requires participation in different issues ranging from casting votes to participating in a technical expert committee or becoming a minister" (Sheshadri, 1976).

Political participation may be defined as those actions of private citizens by which they seek to influence or support government and politics (Milbrath & Goel, 197). This definition is broader than most others, as it includes not only active roles that people pursue in order to influence political outcomes but also ceremonial and support activities. To Almond and Powel, "political participation is the involvement of the members of the society in the decision making process of the system" (Almond & Powelll, 1975). Mc Closky defines, "political participation implies those voluntary activities by which members of a society share in the selection of rulers and directly or indirectly, in the formulation of public policy" (Dowse, 1972). Verba and Pye define it as, "Those activities by private citizens that are more or less directly aimed at influencing the selection of governmental personnel and the actions they take" (Verba & Nie, 1972). Political participation of elected women representatives will be measured in terms of voting, nominations for political posts in parties, pressure groups, election fray, holding positions in political and administrative bodies or institutions, decision making process, attending meetings, raising issues and concern for development and governance.

There is paucity of literature, empirical research findings and data on political participation of women in local governments in post 73rd and 74th Constitutional Amendments Acts as most of the studies are related with empowerment of women trough PRIs. There is lack of comparative study on political participation on elected women representatives of PRIs and ULBs. Thus, the proposed study will be of immense importance for policy implications.

Chapter - 3

Women Empowerment and Panchayati Raj in India

Women empowerment is the buzzword now-a-days. No country can afford development without considering women who constitute about half of its stock of human resource. However, development has bypassed women in India despite worshiping and paying respect to women in mythology and historical texts. Gender disparities vary vastly across cultural, geographical and historical context. India is a large country with vast economic and socio-cultural diversity in its varied regions. The development issues related to women in a large country like India will not only be inappropriate but sometimes even misleading. Women specific and women related legislations have been enacted to safeguard the rights and interest of women, besides protecting against discrimination, violence, and atrocities and also to prevent socially undesirable practices.

Globalization has affected society, culture, economy and polity. The impact of globalization is a mixed bag. It has positive impact on women however; there are some negative impacts also. The positive impacts include creation of employment opportunities for women, strengthening of women's networks and associations for mainstreaming women in development, increase in income, improving the gender participation in decision making process etc. However, it has also caused breaking down of family structure, commodification of women and sexuality, and degradation of socio-cultural value system.

Gender Equality and Empowerment

At the turn of 19th century, industrial revolution brought about radical changes in societies the world over, particularly in the societies which were rooted in the agriculture. One of the radical changes was the removal of manufacture from the households to the factories and shops. The work done at home offered lifelong educational, socialization, communication and residential benefits to the family members. It kept the unemployment and crime rate low. The industrial revolution took away this responsibility from women, brought about a rural urban dichotomy particular in aggregarian society and created demand for some other education agent, outside homes. It resulted in greater segregation and discrimination within all sectors, a majority of women lacking productive and technical skills, science and technology, and extension and training programmes provided primarily to men as women are conceived only as consumers of the industrial revolution (Dhawan, 1995). At the turn of 19th century, communication revolution, which is technology intensive, has brought about another radical transformation again at the home front. Globalization and economic liberalization followed by structural adjustment programmes forced women to involve in economic activities as more salaries are needed just to maintain a house (Dhawan & Singh, 1991).

In India, the plight of women is no better than that of women in other developing countries. Despite the honour and reverence accorded to them as deities in religion and mythology and tribute paid to them as personified in historical monuments, the ground realities have a very different tale to tell. In a patriarchal society like India, there exists the unfounded belief that man is the bread winner of the family. Consequently, the male child gets the best of the limited facilities and resources of the family. The girl child runs the risk of being aborted through the misuse of modern technology of amniocentesis, she is deprived of school education because she has to take care of siblings at home and since she is to be married off soon, investment in her education is considered generally a liability. Despite the fact that women are massively involved in agriculture, food production and the like, their work remains unrecognized. Their activities as producers are not reflected in statistics thus making their contribution invisible. Culturally, in an effort to uphold cultural heritage, the past is glamourized and with it, the trend to equality of women enhancement of their role in development gets inhibited (Pinto, M. 1995).

Women constitute half of the segment of population in India and cannot be afforded to be kept out of the mainstream. Secondly, women are vital and productive workers in India's national economy, and make 1/3rd of the labour force. Thirdly, the poorer the family, the greater is the dependence on women's economic productivity. Fourthly, there is a significant gap between women's potential and actual productivity. Therefore, women will gain proportionally more if investment allocation and development efforts are shifted in their favour. Fifthly, women's earnings have a positive correlation with children's health, nutritional levels and education (Singh and Singh, 2004).

The current wave of globalization has greatly improved, in some respects, the lives of women worldwide, particularly in the developing country like India. Globalization offers women unprecedented opportunities but equally new and unique challenges. Globalization plays a definite role in increasing opportunities for women in the workforce. The modern development of technology offers the possibilities for women to communicate more directly through networking both within and across countries. However, women remain disadvantaged in many areas of their lives, including education, employment, health and rights. In order to create violence and exploitation free environment and to empower women, policy support both from international and national agencies has provided with enforcement of legal provisions, acts and budgetary allocation for schemes and programmes. Ever since, introduction of globalization in 1990s, a few efforts have been made to assess the impact of globalization on women however, there is paucity of empirical research and data on the subject. Most of the studies are concentrating either on empowerment of women or feminist discourse in the context of globalization.

Gender equality and women empowerment are the key terms that defined and determined the direction of diverse discourses on women, nationally and globally. The Beijing conference was the most significant milestone in journey towards ensuring gender equality and enriching pragmatic insights into the issues concerning women empowerment (Singh & Srivastava, 2001). Gender equality is central to realizing the Millennium Development Goals. However, gender discrimination across the life cycle is still prevalent in most of the countries across the globe. In India too, gender discrimination is prevalent in its socio-cultural setup. Gender discrimination is pervasive while the degree and forms of inequality may vary; women and girls are deprived of equal access to resources, opportunities and political power in every region of the world. The oppression of girls and women can include the preference for sons over daughters, limited personnel and professional choices for girls and women, the denial of basic human rights and outright gender based violence (UNICEF, 2007).

Attitudes, belief and practices that serve to exclude women are often deeply entrenched, in many instances closely associated with cultural, social and religious norms. Despite ingrained gender inequality, the status of women has improved in the past decades. The increased awareness of discriminately practices and outcome- including physical and sexual violence, legal and constitutional provisions as well as international pressure has fostered the greater demand for change and women empowerment. Globalization has transformed the structure and patterns of employment. On the one hand, it has created opportunities for employment to women, however, on the other hand, it has created problems to women folk. As majority of the women are employed in unorganized sector which is beyond the protection of labour laws, therefore, the real benefits of globalization could not percolate among women workers. The era of globalization is a process of restructuring of an international sexual division of labour in which third world women serve both as producers of surplus value of cheap manufacture and as objects of (sexual) consumption (through prostitution) for First World men. It is widely believed that globalization widens up the opportunities for women in different sectors but in true sense they rarely stand in the modernization of their economies. On the contrary, as their economies develop new burdens are added upon them. They suffer with inequalities and indignity. As the pace of globalization is spreading fast, industry grows up and men migrate to the cities leaving women behind by leaving the entire burden on the shoulder of women including agriculture, household and social needs. Structural adjustment generated the triple burden for women and globalization has reinforced its consequences. Women have become an integral part of this liberalized labour market, but simultaneously been marginalized within it, as they have to develop strategies for dealing with conflicting demands of fragmented insecure work, domesticity and community participation.

The proportion of women in higher status is one of the key indicators of level of equality between men and women of a society. How women are employed also has important implications for organizational performance and for national economic growth. After looking at the employment hierarchical structure, we find lack of women in the higher rungs. Different scholars give different views as some describe the reason as due to lack of qualified women, which may be due to societal steering mechanisms. And some others have attributed the underrepresentation of women to demand side factors, such as women experience at work, particularly discrimination. Lesser degree of women participation as managers or professionals is a neglected aspect of labour participation in emerging economies. So, it is becoming an important issue to study the low level of women in the higher rungs of employment in general and Indian women in particular as one of the countries where maximum numbers of work force is women.

There are some important approaches of women development given below:

- The welfare approach- until the early 1970s developed policies were directed at women only in the context of their roles as wives and mothers, with a focus on mother and child health and on reducing fertility. It was estimated that the benefits of macroeconomic strategies for growth would automatically trickle down to the poor, and that poor women would benefit as the economic position of their husband improved.
- The WID approach – the rise of women movement in Western Europe and North America, the 1975 UN International year for Women & International Women's Decade [1976-1985] led to the establishment of women ministries in many countries and the institutionalization of Women in Development [WID] policies in governments, donor agencies and NGOs. The aim of the WID was to integrate women into economic development by focusing on income generation projects for women.
- Gender and Development [GAD] this approach originated in academic criticism starting in the mid 1970's in the UK. Based on the concept of gender relations [the socially constructed pattern of relations between men and women] they analyzed how development reshapes these power relations. Drawing on feminist political activism, gender analysts explicitly see women as an agent of change.
- Women and Development [WAD] at the 1975 UN Women's World Conference in Mexico City the feminist approaches of predominantly white women from the north aimed at gender equality were rejected by many women in the South who argued that the development model itself lacked the perspective of developing countries. They saw overcoming poverty and the effects of colonialism as more important than equality.
- The efficiency approach - the strategy under this approach was to argue that, in the context of structural adjustment programmes [SAPs], gender analysis made good economic sense. It was recognized the understanding men and women, roles and responsibilities as part of the planning of development interventions improved project effectiveness.
- The empowerment approach in the 1980s, empowerment was regarded as a weapon for the weak, best wielded through grassroots

and participatory activities. However, empowerment has many meanings and by mid 1990,s some mainstream development agencies has begun to adopt the term (Jane, 2002).

- Gender and the Environment [GED] this approach was based on eco feminist views, especially those of Vandana Shiva, which made an essentialist link between women and the environment and encouraged environmental programmes to focus on women's roles (Shiva, Vandana).
- Mainstreaming gender equality; the term 'gender mainstreaming' came into wide spread use with the adoption of the Platform for Action at the 1995 UN Forth World Conference on Women held in Beijing. The 189 governments represented in Beijing unanimously affirmed that the advancement of women and the achievement of equality with men are matters of fundamental human rights and therefore a prerequisite for social justice. Mainstreaming gender equality tries to ensure that women's as well as men, concern and experiences are integral to the design, implementation, monitoring and evaluation of all projects so that gender inequality is not perpetuated. It attempts to overcome the common problem of 'policy evaporation's the implementation and impact of development projects fails to reflect policy commitments (Helan, 2001).

In the late 1990s donor-supported development shifted away from discrete project interventions to general poverty elimination, which potentially provides an ideal context for gender mainstreaming. Attention is only just beginning to be paid to the gender dimensions of poverty alleviation (Narayan and Petesch, 2002). The Millennium Declaration signed at the United Nations Millennium Summit in 2000 sets out the United Nations goals for the next decade. These goals come from the resolutions of the various world conferences organized by the United Nations during the 1990s reaching these goals will not be easy but they do set standards which can be monitored (UNDP, 2003). The Beijing Platform for Action prioritized gender mainstreaming as the mechanism to achieve gender equality. Mainstreaming a gender perspective is the process of assessing the implications for women and men of any planned action including legislation, policies or programmes, in all areas and at all levels (Moser and Moser, 2006). Gender mainstreaming policies share the following six key components viz.. (1) a dual strategy of mainstreaming gender combined with targeted actions for gender equality; (2) gender analysis; (3) a combined approach to responsibilities, where all staff share responsibility, but are supported by gender specialist; (4) gender training; and (5) support to women's decision making and empowerment; and (6) monitoring and evaluation.

Women's development has come a long way from the earlier welfare orientation. In the welfare approach, women were taken as vulnerable sections of the population, whose situation could be ameliorated through the provision of support services like health, nutrition and child care. Women's development has been looked at variously from perspectives that have followed the welfare approach. The present approach of empowerment looks at unequal gender and power relations and use conscientisation, mobilization, solidarity and collective action as the solution (Chart-3.1).

Chart: 3.1. Different Perspectives to Women's Development

Type of Project goal	*Concepts*		*Type of developmental interventions*
	Concept of the problem	*Concept of the solution*	
Welfare	Women's poverty, women's special needs, women as a vulnerable groups, women's lower socio-economic status	Provision of support services of health, nutrition, child care	Build maternity clinics, health clinics, immunization, health education, nutrition education
Economic self-reliance	Women as under-employed, unproductive, dependent, lacking in productive skills	Promote self reliance and inter-dependence, provide productive skills, encourage women's productive enterprises	Income generating projects for women, women's clubs, soap making, school uniform making etc.
Efficiency	Women as previously overlooked resource in development planning, women as under developed human capital	Identify actual productive roles of women, support women with skills, training and improved technology, invest in previously over looked resource	Integration of women in development planning, mainstreaming of women's development, extension advice for women farmers, appropriate technology for women, increase women's access to factors of production
Equality	Structure of inequality, discrimination against women in schooling, credit, access to land	Equality of opportunities for women in schooling, access to factors of production	Affirmative action to promote equal opportunity, revise development planning so that women are equal partners and beneficiaries in development process.
Empowerment	Unequal gender power relations, the patriarchy, patriarchal resistance	Conscientisation, mobilization, solidarity, collective action	Grass roots projects, support for women's collective action, project concerned with democratization and political action

Source: UNICEF, based on Moser, in ICECD, Making Development Gender Sensitive, a Guide for Trainers, Ahmadabad, ICECD.

There has been paradigm shift from a welfare orientation to an empowerment approach. This has further led to the emerging concept of engendering development in order to ensure gender equity, gender mainstreaming and women-centric governance. Though, India is among the most complex democracy in the world, with a long history of commitments to women's welfare and empowerment through constitutional provisions, legislation, policies and plans even while deep levels of structural gender bias persists within families, societies and economies. There are formidable opportunities and challenges, including continued high rate of economic growth in the phase of declining sex ratio, decreasing energy and natural resources, increasing income inequality and an urban rural divide. Thus, gender equality has become a core prerequisite for sustainable and equitable economic growth (National Alliance of Women, 2008). Women are major contributors to the India's economy and therefore empowerment of women is essential for distributive justice and national growth. Engendering growth model and development plans may create opportunities for women in their mainstreaming in development process and governance. The growth models and development planning requires the suitable mechanism which is able to address the gender concerns at all stages and policy commitments along with budgetary support for them.

12th Five Year Plan has recognized the primacy of India's women and children who constitute about 70 percent of population. The Plan envisages the engendering of development planning and making it more child-centric. High priority has been given to women and children from the poorest communities, from the most deprived socio-religious communities, such as Scheduled Caste, Scheduled Tribes, particularly vulnerable Tribal communities and others. The key elements for gender equity to be addressed in the 12th Five Year Plan include economic empowerment, social and physical infrastructure, enabling legislations, women's participation in governance, inclusiveness of all categories of women, engendering policies and programmes, and mainstreaming women through gender budgeting. Women are major contributors to India's economy and an important constituent of development. Their empowerment is essential for distributive justice and for the nation's growth. Engendering the nation's development plan and processes means recognizing that women and men are socialized differently and Thus, gender as a macroeconomic variable, needs to be incorporated into the growth model. Engendering the growth model requires that women be perceived as producers of economic groups and of non-economic groups that contributes to development. The growth model in the planning process assumes three sources of growth viz., capital, labour and technology. However this excludes natural capital. An engender plan would include a gender dimension in all macro policies – fiscal, trade, agriculture, industry, infrastructure, labour and employment. In past, government of India has undertaken a large number of schemes aimed at the socio-economic development of women under various Five Year Plans. Development of women in the First Five Year Plan (1951- 56) was clubbed with the welfare of disadvantaged group like destitute, disabled, aged, etc. The Second to Fifth Plan (1956-79) continue to reflect the same welfare approach besides giving priority to women's education and launching measures to improve maternal and child health services, supplementary feeding for children, and expectant and nursing mother. Sixth Plan (1980-85) has marked a clear shift in its approach, from welfare to development oriented plans towards women. Seventh Plan (1985-90) aimed at raising women's economic and social status and bringing them into the mainstream of the national development. Eighth Plan (1992-97) focuses on human development with special reference to women. The Ninth Plan (1997-2002) made significant changes in the conceptual strategy of planning for women development. The Tenth Plan (2002-07) continued with its strategy of empowering women as agent of social change and development. The Eleventh Five Year Plan has highly emphasized on synergic approach of gender budget and gender mainstreaming process for ensuring gender empowerment and equity. The Twelfth Five Year Plan recognizes the primacy of India's women and children, who constitute over 70 per cent of India's population. The plan strategy of inclusion envisages the engendering of development planning and making it more child-centric. Structural transformation is called for not only in the women and child related direct policy and programme interventions, but also more generally in the policies and programmes of the many sectors that impact upon women and children especially those from the weaker sections or whose individual circumstances make them the most vulnerable (Chart 3.2).

Chart: 3.2. Gender Development in Indian Planning

First Five Year Plan (1951-56)	Development of women was clubbed with the welfare of the disadvantaged groups like destitute, disabled, aged, etc.
Second to Fifth Five Year Plans (1956-79)	Welfare approach, besides giving priority to women's education, improved maternal and child health services, supplementary feeding for children and expectant and nursing mothers.
Sixth Five Year Plan (1980-85)	Shift in the approach from 'welfare' to 'development' of women. Multi-disciplinary approach with thrust on health, education and employment.
Seventh Five Year Plan (1985-90)	Aimed at raising women's economic and social status and bringing them into the mainstream of national development. The thrust was on generation of both skilled and unskilled employment through proper education and vocational training.

(Contd...)

Eighth Five Year Plan (1992-97)	Emphasis on the development of women.
Ninth Five Year Plan (1997-2002)	Attempted 'Empowerment of Women'. The Plan also aimed at 'convergence of existing services' available in both women-specific and women-related sectors.
Tenth Five Year Plan (2002-07)	Continues with the strategy of "Empowering Women" as an agent of social change and development through Social Empowerment, Economic Empowerment and Gender Justice.
Eleventh Five Year Plan (2007-2012)	The plan proposes to undertake special measures for gender empowerment and equity. The Ministry of Women and Child Development would make synergic use of gender budget and gender mainstreaming process.
Twelfth Five Year Plan (2012-2017)	Engendering of development planning and making it more child-centric.

Source: Planning Commission, Govt. of India.

Women's development has come a long way from the earlier welfare orientation. In the welfare approach, women were taken as vulnerable sections of the population, whose situation could be ameliorated through the provision of support services like health, nutrition and child care. Women's development has been looked at variously from perspectives that have followed the welfare approach. The present approach of empowerment looks at unequal gender and power relations and use conscientisation, mobilization, solidarity and collective action as the solution (Chart 3.3).

Chart: 3.3 Different Aspects of Development in Context of Gender

CULTURAL	*LEGAL*	*POLITICAL*	*ECONOMIC*	*SOCIAL*
• Respect of rights of indigenous and traditional people • Participation in local resource management • Inclusion of indigenous knowledge	• Awareness of rights • Decentralization • Mainstreaming gender perspectives • Decision making	• Gender justice, elimination of all forms of gender discrimination	• Poverty Eradication • Micro-credit • Women and Economy • Globalization • Women and Agriculture • Women and Industry • Support services	• Education • Health • Nutrition • Drinking water • Sanitation • Housing and Shelter • Environment

Source: Singh, 2009.

The Millennium Declaration signed at the United Nations Millennium Summit in 2000 sets out the United Nations goals for the next decade. These goals come from the resolutions of the various world conferences organized by the United Nations during the 1990s reaching these goals will not be easy but they do set standards which can be monitored (UNDP,

2003). The Beijing Platform for Action prioritized gender mainstreaming as the mechanism to achieve gender equality. Mainstreaming a gender perspective is the process of assessing the implications for women and men of any planned action including legislation, policies or programmes, in all areas and at all levels (Moser and Moser, 2006). Empowerment of all women and girls is to be realized through sustainable development. Sustainable development depends on an equitable distribution of resources and it cannot be achieved without gender equality. Gender equity is the process of allocating resources, programs, and decision making fairly to both males and females without any discrimination on the basis of sex…and addressing any imbalances in the benefits available to males and females. Sustainable Development Goals were born at the United Nations Conference on Sustainable Development, Rio+20, in 2012. The objective of SDGs was to provide a group of universally applicable goals that balances the three dimensions of sustainable development that are environmental, social, and economic. The Sustainable Development Goals (SDGs) are based on the Millennium Development Goals (MDGs). The 17 Sustainable Development Goals and 169 targets decided at the United Nations Headquarters in New York from 25-27 September 2015, demonstrate the scale and ambition of the new universal Agenda. The new SDGs are more broad than the MDGs, addressing the root causes of poverty and the universal need for development that works for all people. The specific targets of SDGs are to be achieved by 2030. The SDGs are based on the Millennium Development Goals (MDGs). However, contrarily to the MDGs that were intended for action in developing countries only, the SDGs apply to all countries. Sustainable development cannot be achieved without gender equality (Development Alternatives, 2015).

The following target has been enclosed to attain gender equality and empowerment of all women and girls (U N. Women, 2015):

- End all forms of discrimination against all women and girls at all places;
- To abolish all forms of violence against women and girls in the public and private spheres, including trafficking, sexual abuse and other types of exploitation;
- Eliminate all harmful traditional practices, such as child, early and forced marriages and female genital mutilation;
- Value the unpaid care and domestic work through the provision of public services, infrastructure and social protection policies/ schemes and the promotion of shared responsibility within the household and the family;

- To ensure that women practice full and effective participation and equal opportunities for leadership at all levels of decision-making in political, economic and public realms of life;
- To assure Universal access to sexual and reproductive health and rights.

Gender Mainstreaming

Policy approaches to women and development in India have changed over the years of planned development. However, the shift from 'welfare' to an 'empowerment' approach has remained more in the realm of the rhetoric. The approach to the Twelfth Plan also exhibits insufficient awareness of the specific problems of women, their unpaid labour and their distinctive economic contribution to the nation's economy. Thus, the major shift through this initiative was to move the engendering of public policy into the macroeconomic space (Government of India, 2010). The policy approach underlying both the Eleventh and Twelfth plans expects to promote economic growth through creating opportunities for the entrepreneurial class by liberalizing domestic and global markets. This framework – in which Gross Domestic Product (GDP) growth is the relevant indicator and 'a dynamic private sector' is seen as the main instrument for its expansion – gives insufficient importance to employment intensive activities and conditions of existence for the majority of workers. The inclusion of the excluded or marginalized socio-economic groups is expected to occur through a trickling down of growth, expansion of productive employment in the economy, as well as implementation of flagship and other targeted programmes to be financed by the increased revenues of the government resulting from high growth rates. However, the direction of macroeconomic and growth policies is one that continuously undermines the possibility of better employment creation for greater numbers. This in turn permeates and infects all the other aspects of the Approach such that the basic objective of making growth "more inclusive" is unlikely to be met (UNIFEM, 2013) . The strategies for growth proposed in the Approach to the Twelfth Plan appear to be formulated with little consideration for the needs and roles of large sections of the population of the country and especially of poor women. This document aims to highlight some of these gaps in the overall design of the proposed approach to planning and to suggest ways of making economic growth during the Twelfth Plan truly more inclusive.

There is little evidence to show that the accelerated growth rate of the economy during the Eleventh Plan led to any significant achievement of inclusion. It deflects responsibility for achieving inclusiveness by stating that "success depends not only on introducing new policies and government programmes, but on institutional and attitudinal changes, which take time". Inclusiveness has remained elusive. Even the limited focus given to inclusion and equity in the Eleventh Plan appears to have been jettisoned in the Twelfth Plan Approach, which focuses narrowly only on growth per se, assuming growth will ensure an improvement in the lives of people overall. The paragraphs on inclusion in the Introduction to the Approach Paper are particularly weak as they remain at the level of general intentions. There is lack of clarity regarding how inclusion will occur (UNIFEM, 2013).

In order to ensure inclusive growth, it is essential that all potential workers find remunerative employment in the mainstream of development. *Generating productive work has to be an integral part of the plan model.* It is now officially acknowledged (NCUES, 2007) that economic 'development' has not just witnessed the growth of the informal sector and of those being employed informally, but also the phenomenon of the 'informalization of the formal sector'. Further, there is remarkable consistency in the manner in which larger numbers of women and their 'work' either become invisible in data systems or get captured in categories that fall outside the purview of protective legislation. The organized or formal economy supposedly enjoys the protection of labour laws with some modicum of social security, but even this apparent protection is elusive. The National Commission for Enterprises in the Unorganized Sector (2009) estimated the effectiveness of the coverage of important labour laws for the year 1999-2000. Among other things, this exercise revealed that the effectiveness of coverage as far as the Maternity Benefit Act, 1961 was concerned was only 16 per cent. The International Labour Organization's recently concluded evaluation of maternity benefit schemes in India, carried this exercise further and revealed the manner in which eligible women workers were denied maternity benefits statutorily due to them (Lingan and Krishnaraj, 2010).

The manufacturing sector currently poses a serious problem for the Indian economy. Despite rapid growth in production during the last five years, its contribution to the national economy still remains relatively small and it has failed to generate additional decent employment. Especially for women, manufacturing employment actually shrank in this period. These trends are contrary to the world-wide pattern of economic development. While mentioning the need for generating employment in manufacturing, the Approach Paper for Twelfth Plan does not explore the sector's potential for doing so, besides making a 'brave' assumption that an additional hundred million decent jobs will be created by 2025, when only five million jobs were added to manufacturing in the whole decade preceding i.e. 1999-2000 to 2009-10. There was an increase in manufacturing employment from 44 to 55 million between 1999-2000 and 2004-05, but it fell to 50 million in 2010. Instead of recognizing this reality, the paper goes on to focus only on ways of enhancing the sector's contribution to the GDP and neglects other concerns. Methods by which such a massive number of jobs are to be created remain unaddressed. Manufacturing employment actually declined in the period 2004-05 to 2009-10, even though manufacturing output grew at an annual compound rate of more than 8 per cent over the period.

The Approach Paper for Twelfth Plan mentions the setting up of a high level National Transport Development Policy Committee to develop a transport policy going up to 2030, which will facilitate an efficient expansion of the transportation network in a manner that would help to minimize energy use and would place special attention on competitive pricing and coordination between alternative modes of transport. However, transport needs to be viewed not merely as a support for rapid growth, but also as an agent for change and development, for increasing the physical and societal mobility of people, especially women. Women's inclusion in developmental activities rests critically on their mobility. Needless to state, the National Transport Policy has to keep women's needs in mind. Gendered infrastruc-tural empowerment is obvious in the several levels of interconnections.

There are several ways in which gender sensitive policies can be implemented in the context of investment in infrastructure. These include pre-project rapid gender assessment surveys; gender-sensitive project coordination team and appropriate institutional structures; participatory project planning and implementation with women and men in communities, including procurement activities; women's participation and decision-making in community infrastructure management; women's participation in generating and operating maintenance funds; promotion of local cooperatives and SHGs for provision of materials; special concessions for women and child-headed households, pregnant women, MGNREGA households; financial resources for capacity building and training of local authorities; dissemination of guidelines in local languages for operation, management, and maintenance of public infrastructure; collection of sex disaggregated data; systematic institutionalized evaluation through use of appropriate gender budgeting tools for each project and sub-sector; formation of sector-wise multi-agency steering committees; systematic policy consultation and support for identifying gaps, strategizing action plans, and gender mainstreaming; development of appropriate infrastructure in the form of legal mechanisms and services; expansion of public sector; and extension of gendered regulation in private sector with cautious use of Public Private Partnership in building infrastructure (UNIFEM, 2013).

There is need for recognizing the critical care work provided by women, that saves the public health system both time and cost. The primary responsibility of care-giving within the home lies with women. This needs to be recognized and support provided to alleviate the difficulties, drudgery and depression that surround this role. The burden on home-based care givers must be reduced by strengthening primary health centres and public hospitals, community care homes and hospices. India's urban population has increased from 285 million in 2001 to almost 400 million in 2011. The Approach Paper for Twelfth Plan states that by 2030, out of a total projected population of 1.4 billion, over 600 million people may be living in urban areas. The process of urbanization is a natural process associated with growth and that agglomeration and densification of economic activities in urban conglomerations stimulates economic efficiencies and provides more opportunities for earning livelihoods; possibilities for entrepreneurship and employment and "this enables faster inclusion of more people in the growth process and is therefore more inclusive." Most workers in urban areas are working in the informal economy. An analysis of the NSS 2004-2005 data shows that 80 percent of the total urban working population is informally employed. Informal employment is higher for women than for men. About 85 percent of all women workers are informally employed as compared to 79 percent of all male workers. One reason why the number of informal workers has increased is because of the growing 'informalization' of the formal sector, with 34 percent of the formal enterprises employing informal workers in the form of contract workers or casual labour. Among the self employed, most of the workers would be in a "vulnerable" category, being either own account workers such as street vendors or family helpers. The better-off, employer categories who employ one or more employees are only 5 percent of the self employed. For women, the main areas of work are home-based work and domestic work. More than 16 percent of the women were hired by households as domestic workers – double the percentage in 1999-2000; whereas over 38 per cent of women were home-based workers, a category of work that has grown substantially in 2009-10 (UNIFEM, 2013).

The role of governance, in particular local governance, in which women can play an active role in developmental planning, given their political presence is critical in this convergence. Women's participation as elected representatives in local bodies has been noteworthy. Hence, the strengthening of these agencies' roles and powers, especially for implementing the 'inclusive' programmes at the grassroots level would be enabling for women led governance factored in. Needless to state, it is the combined effect of these inclusive programmes that can ameliorate much of the rural deprivation, in particular for women who perform some of these tasks.

Engendering Development

The issue of engendering development and women empowerment has been in the central stage with the shifting of paradigm of development and governance at the global level and particularly in India. Gender budgeting has emerged as an important instrument for gender mainstream and women empowerment across the globe. It has been well recognized by the policy makers and feminist economists that gender budgeting is imperative for gender equality and engendering development planning. Gender budgeting refers to the systematic examination of the budget programmes and policies for the impact on women. Studies show that programmes and policies design to improve women's economic opportunities lead to higher rates of economic growth. Gender budgeting has gained prominence in the policy circles in the recent years. In view of the growing importance of the gender budgeting, the present study purports to critically review the plans, policies, programmes and schemes and also to examine union budgets through gender lens.

Women are major contributors to India's economy and important constituent of development. Their empowerment is essential for distributive justice for the nation's growth. Engendering national development plans is imperative for gender mainstreaming and their empowerment. Engendered development plans would include a gender dimension in all macro policies and budgetary support for their implementation. Engendering public policy and gender budgeting are the major gender commitments by Government of India. Gender budgeting has three basic dimensions. One, the empowerment has to be holistic and it should cover political, social and economic implications for women. It should be universal in terms of equal opportunities. The second dimension is that it should be participative and inclusive. This requires that planning, policy and implementation process should have a bottom to top approach, where women have a voice from the gross roots to the highest echelons of power. The third dimension of gender budgeting is the need for convergence. Women's needs are multi-dimensional – access to health and nutrition, water and sanitation, asset based marketing, credit, technology, education and skills, political participation etc. Thus, convergence of development policies, programmes, schemes and institutional resources is imperative for engendering and inclusive development. There is also the need for revision in existing urban development schemes and programmes so that gender issues may be incorporated and their concerns are effectively addressed.

As per Census 2011, the population of India is more than 121 Crore with 48.5 percent females, 949 female to 1000 males in rural India against 929 females to 1000 males in urban India. As per SRS 2016, the infant mortality rate has decreased from 37 in 2015 to 34 in 2016. The maternal mortality rate has declined significantly from 301 in 2001-2003 to 130 in 2014-16. Educational attainment is the first and foremost step towards improving quality of life, awareness level and also level of skill of people in the society. Better literacy and educational level definitely have a positive impact on overall development and productivity. India has enacted 'Right to Education' to ensure free and compulsory Education for children in the age group 6-14 years. Literacy and level of education are basic indicators of the level of development achieved by a society. Higher levels of education and literacy, particularly of female literacy, lead to a greater awareness and also contributes in improvement of economic and social conditions. It acts as a catalyst for social upliftment enhancing the returns on investment made in almost every aspect of development effort, be it population control, health, hygiene, environmental degradation control, employment of weaker sections of the society.

As per 2011 census, literacy rate in India has been reported as 72.98 percent with a 13 percent increase to that in 2001, whereas the hike is high for rural women at 20 percent in the last decade, which may be attributed to literacy mission of Government of India. The female literacy rate according to the 2011 census is 64.63 percent whereas the male literacy rate is over 80 percent. As per 2011 census, the highest female literacy rate is in Kerala (92.1 percent) followed by Mizoram (89.3 percent) and Lakshadweep (87.9 percent). Similar results are found in male literacy with Kerala (96.1 percent), Mizoram (93.7 percent) and Lakshadweep (91.8 percent). As per MHRD data, there is a declining trend in Gross Enrolment Ratio (GER) for primary classes (Class I to V) for both females and males. However, there is upward trend in for upper primary and higher secondary classes for both male and females. The number of females per 100 males enrolled in different stages like secondary, senior secondary and higher education are at 91, 90 and 86 respectively.

Enhancing women's participation in economic activities is very critical not only for achieving poverty reduction and economic development but it also crucial for over all social development. Reducing gender gap in participation in economic activities contributes towards many other benefit of economic prosperity such as improvement in child survival, overall family health, reduction in fertility etc. The economic activities are broadly classified as organized and unorganized, each of which may be in the formal or informal sector. Participation of women in economic activities in formal sectors of industries, services and agricultural sector is measurable, but activities of women in informal sectors such as house works, training and education of children, activities in agricultural sectors and household services are still not measured. Women constitute roughly half of the economically active population, but their contribution to economic activity is far below the potential. Unlocking this large potential could work as catalyst in achieving goals as set under Sustainable Development Goals. As per Census 2011, the workforce participation rate for females is 25.51 percent against 53.26 percent for males. Rural sector has a better female workforce participation rate of 30.02 percent compared with 53.03 percent for males whereas for urban sector. Rural India has more than 50 percent workers in self-employed category, whereas urban India has more than 40 percent workers in self-employed and regular wage categories as per NSS 68th Round , 2011-12.

Political Status of Women

Political participation is the hallmark of a democratic setup. Nature, success and effectiveness of democracy largely depend on the extent to which equal, effective and actual participation is provided by the system to all its citizens. As women comprise about half of the population, this section of society requires due attention in the system and a due share in process. Citizens' active participation in political affairs in a democracy is crucial and necessary because it provides legitimacy to the system and also strengthens the democratic fabric (Palmer, 1976). Democracy will fail in its objectives if women citizens lack equal opportunity to participate in the governmental decision-making process. They are to be equal partners in the nation-building and political development.

Political democracy requires at least a minimum of people's participation in the decision making process. Citizens' participation in political affairs is important because a situation which results in high participation by members of a group normally has higher potential for democracy (Lipset, 1973). Norman D. Palmer defines political participation as the involvement of citizens in such political activities, which directly or indirectly influence the behaviour and actions of decision-makers (Palmer, 1976). It may be viewed as any "Voluntary action, successful or unsuccessful, organized or unorganized, episodic or continuous, employing legitimate or illegitimate methods, intended to influence the choice of public policies, the administration of public affairs, or the choices of political leaders at any level of government, local or national" (Weiner, 1976).

It may be pointed out that all citizens do not participate equally or in the same manner in any political process. The political culture of a society greatly influences the nature of political participation of individuals. The real purpose and impact of participation is to make the citizen not a passive spectator but an agent in politics, to enable him to show his disagreement as much as to endorse what is proposed, as much to scotch Initiatives as to launch them, as much to revise, criticize and block as to push, prod and hasten (Mount, 1974). However, if political participation is to have any concrete meaning, particularly in a democratic setup, people should directly or indirectly take part in the decision-making processes which affect their day to day life. Political participation of women in India is reported to be low at all levels of political and administrative institutions, however, there has been increasing trend in participation of women in local governments , both in PRIs and ULBs . This is because of the fact that one third seats of PRIs and ULBs have been reserved for women. Though, there has been a slight decrease in female voting in 2004 General Election as compared to 1999, participation in the electoral process as voters has steadily increased from 46.6 percent in 1962 to around 55.8 percent in 2009. The difference in voter turnout among men and women that was as wide as 16.7 percent in 1962 as narrowed down to 4.4 percent in 2009. Data reveals that women living in rural areas of India vote higher as compared to those living in urban location, as rural women are ahead by 5 percentage points in voting in 2004 in General Elections. Similarly, women located in the Southern and Eastern Region of India, exercise their ballot options more as compared to women residing in the Western and Northern regions of the country. Thus, more women from Southern and Eastern regions voted in 2004 as compared with their counterparts residing in the other two regions of India. Women in India are still not well represented in political life as Members in Parliament and in some State Legislative Assemblies that would require them to be active in the public sphere. Women's representation in Lok Sabha since the First General Elections reveals that they continue to be grossly excluded from electoral participation at the top even after so many years of Independence. In 1952, they constituted 4.4 percent of total members in the Lower House which has increased to around 11 percent in 2009 and 2014, but it is still below the world average of 20 percent. The Rajya Sabha does not fair much better, with 27 women members comprising 11.5 percent of total membership in 2013 (Table 3.1).

Table: 3.1 Representation of Women in Lower House of Indian Parliament

Lok Sabha	*Total Number of Seats (Election Held)*	*Number of Women Members Who Won*	*Percentage of the Total*
First (1952)	489	22	4.4
Second (1957)	494	27	5.4
Third (1962)	494	34	6.7
Fourth (1967)	523	31	5.9
Fifth (1971)	521	22	4.2
Sixth (1977)	544	19	3.4
Seventh (1980)	544	28	5.1
Eighth (1984)	544	44	8.1
Ninth (1989)	529	28	5.3
Tenth (1991)	509	36	7.0
Eleventh (1996)	541	40*	7.4
Twelfth (1998)	545	44*	8.0
Thirteenth (1999)	543	48*	8.8
Fourteenth (2004)	543	45*	8.1
Fifteenth (2009)	543	59	10.9
Sixteenth (2014)	543	62	11.0
Seventieth (2019)	543	78	14.4

* Including one nominated member.

Source: National Election Study, CSDS Data Unit, Delhi.

Women in India are still not well represented in political life as Members in Parliament and in some State Legislative Assemblies that would require them to be active in the public sphere. Women's representation in Lok Sabha since the First General Elections reveals that they continue to be grossly excluded from electoral participation at the top even after so many years of Independence. In 1952, they constituted 4.4 percent of total members in the Lower House which has increased to around 11 percent in 2009 and 2014, but it is still below the world average of 20 percent. The Rajya Sabha does not fair much better, with 27 women members comprising 11.5 percent of total membership in 2013. The number of women ticket holders from state parties felt sharply from 66 in 2004 to 27 in 2009. For national parties, the number of women candidates actually increased from 110 to134 but nearly 60 percent of the increase is attributed to BJP alone. While the Congress's number of women candidates reduced marginally, the BJP fielded 50 percent more women than it did in 2004. The party with highest representation of women was All India Trinamul Congress with 18.5 percent women candidates. Nationalist Congress Party provided about 10 percent tickets to female candidates.

The 16th Lok Sabha is under presented by women; though it is likely to have the highest ever number of them. Of the 543 MPs, only 62 constituting 11 per cent are women. This is a negligible improvement from 2009, when

61 women candidates were elected to the Lower House. However, the Bhartiya Janata Party scores to the highest number of women MPs – out of 58, 28 are from BJP, the party had fielded 35 women candidates. The Trinamul Congress comes second with 11 of its 24 candidates emerging victorious. Out of total 8163 candidates, 636 women contested election across the country. In 2009 556 (6.9 percent) women candidates had contested out of a total of 8070 candidates. The representation of women MPs has been reported high in West Bengal (29 percent) followed by Uttarakhand (20 percent), Madhya Pradesh (17 percent), Jammu and Kashmir (17 percent), Uttar Pradesh (16 percent), Gujarat (15 percent), Delhi (14 percent) and Assam (14 percent) (Table 3.2.

Table: 3.2 Women Representation in Parliament in 2014

State	*Number of Women MPs*	*Total Number of MPS*	*per cent of Women MPs*
West Bengal	12	42	29.00
Uttarakhand	1	5	20.00
Madhya Pradesh	5	29	17.00
Jammu & Kashmir	1	6	17.00
Uttar Pradesh	13	80	16.00
Gujarat	4	26	15.00
Delhi	1	7	14.00
Assam	2	14	14.00
Maharashtra	5	48	10.00
Tamil Nadu	4	39	10.00
Orissa	2	21	10.00
Bihar	3	40	8.00
Punjab	1	13	8.00
Andhra Pradesh	3	42	7.00
Kerala	1	20	5.00
Rajasthan	1	25	4.00
Karnataka	1	28	4.00
Chandigarh	1	1	100.00
Total	61	543	11.00

Source: Times of India, May 17, 2014.

Even at the second strata of women's participation in electoral process as candidates in elections, there are inherent barriers and restrictions imposed by political parties that severely restrict their chances of candidature. This becomes fairly evident by numerical analysis of the number of seats allotted to women by 4 prominent political parties in the last three General Elections. The number of women candidates who contested the elections has increased and almost double from 284 in General Elections held in 1999 to 566 in the General Elections of 2004, but the number of women candidates fielded by National Parties except for BJP, has remained almost the same during this intervening period. Out of 245 seats in Rajya Sabha, there were 29 women during 2014. Thus, women constituted about 12 percent in Rajya Sabha. The number of women in Rajya Sabha was recorded highest in 1990 (38) followed by 2014 (29). The proportion of women in Rajya Sabha was recorded highest in 1990 (15.5 percent) followed by 2014 (11.83 percent) and 1985 (11.4 percent).

Representation of women in Lok Sabha during 2014 was reported highest from the states of West Bengal followed by Uttarakhand, Jammu and Kashmir, Madhya Pradesh, Uttar Pradesh and Gujarat. Representation of women in State Assembly was recorded highest in Bihar (15 percent) followed by Rajasthan (14 percent), Madhya Pradesh (13 percent), Punjab (12 percent), West Bengal (12 percent), Assam (12 percent) and Chhattisgarh (11 percent). Women representation in Panchayati Raj Institutions was reported highest in Jharkhand (58.6 percent), Uttarakhand (56.1 percent), Chhattisgarh (54.5 percent), Kerala (51.9 percent) and Madhya Pradesh (50.5 percent). It is to be noted that the states like Bihar, Jharkhand, Chhattisgarh, Madhya Pradesh, Uttarakhand, Himachal Pradesh, Rajasthan, Kerala and Maharashtra have already made 50 percent reservation for women in PRIs and Urban Local Governments. Women representation in State Legislative Assemblies exceeds from 14 percent. It is only in two states of Bihar and Rajasthan where number of women legislators is 14 per cent. Mizoram, Nagaland and Pondicherry are such types of states where no women legislator enter in the House. Women representation in the House has been found low in the state of Arunachal Pradesh, Goa, Delhi, Jammu and Kashmir, Karnataka, Maharashtra, Meghalaya and Orissa. However, it has been found significant in the states of Bihar, Chhattisgarh, Haryana, Gujarat, Himachal Pradesh, Madhya Pradesh, Punjab, Rajasthan and West Bengal.

During Lok Sabha election in 2019, 724 women candidates were in election fray. More than 300 women candidates were provided party tickets by BJP alone. Congress party fielded 52 women candidates while YSRCP and Trinamool provided tickets to 22 women, each, in the election. However, winning ratio was recorded high for BJD (41.67 percent), followed by Trinamool (40.91 percent and YSRCP (18.18 percent). Out of 78 elected women, 11 women, each, were from Uttar Pradesh and West Bengal. Odisha represented 7 women while Maharashtra sent 8 women in lower house of Parliament.

Women representation in State Legislative Assemblies exceeds from 14 percent. It is only in two states of Bihar and Rajasthan where number of women legislators is 14 percent. Mizoram, Nagaland and Pondicherry are such types of states where no women legislator enter in the House. Women representation in the House has been found low in the state of Arunachal Pradesh, Goa, Delhi, Jammu and Kashmir, Karnataka, Maharashtra, Meghalaya and Orissa. However, it has been found significant in the states of Bihar, Chhattisgarh, Haryana, Gujarat, Himachal Pradesh, Madhya Pradesh, Punjab, Rajasthan and West Bengal. Representation of women in State Assemblies is still less. Analysis from the available data shows that in elections held during 2013 to 2017 for various State Legislative Assemblies, percentage of women representation is only as high as 14 percent (in Bihar, Haryana & Rajasthan). On an average at all India level, in 2017, 9 percent of the State Assembly members and 5 percent of the State Council members were women (Table 3.3).

Table: 3.3 Representation of Women in State Legislative Assemblies

State	*Male*	*Female*	*Total Members*
Andhra Pradesh	258 (88.35%)	34 |(11.65%)	292 (100%)
Arunachal Pradesh	58 (96.67%)	2 (3.33%)	60 (100%)
Assam	112 (88.89%)	14 (11.11%)	126 (100%)
Bihar	209 (86.00%)	34 (14.00%)	243 (100%)
Chhattisgarh	79 (87.88%)	11 (12.22%)	90 (100%)
Delhi	67 (95.71%)	3 (4.29%)	70 (100%)
Goa	30 (97.5%)	1 (2.60%)	40 (100%)
Gujarat	166 (91.21%)	16 (8.79%)	182 (100 %)
Haryana	81 (90.00%)	9 (10.0%)	90 (100%)
Himachal Pradesh	63 (92.65%)	50 (7.35%)	68 (100%)
Jammu and Kashmir	84 (96.55%)	3 (3.45%)	87 (100%)
Jharkhand	73 (90.12%)	8 (9.88%)	81 (100%)
Karnataka	221 (98.66 %)	3 (1.34%)	224 (100%)
Kerala	133 (95.00%)	7 (5.00%)	140 (100%)
Madhya Pradesh	205 (89.13%)	25 (10.87%)	230 (100%)
Maharashtra	277 (96.18%)	11 (3.82%)	288 (100%)
Manipur	57 (95.00%)	3 (5.00%)	60 (100%)
Meghalaya	58 (98.30%)	1 (2.70%)	59 (100%)
Mizoram	40 (100%)	0	40 (100%)
Nagaland	60 (100%)	0	60 (100 %)
Orissa	140 (95.24%)	7 (4.76%)	147 (100%)
Punjab	103 (88.03%)	14 (11.97%)	117 (100%)
Puducherry	30 (100%)	0	30 (100%)
Rajasthan	172 (86.00%)	28 (14.00%)	200 (100%)
Sikkim	28 (87.5%)	4 (12.50%)	32 (100%)
Tamil Nadu	217 (92.73%)	17 (7.27%)	234 (100%)
Tripura	57 (95.00%)	3 (5.00%)	60 (100%)

(Contd...)

Uttar Pradesh	368 (91.31%)	35 (8.69%)	403 (100%)
Uttarakhand	65 (92.86%)	5 (7.14%)	70 (100%)
West Bengal	260 (88.43%)	34 (11.57%)	294 (100%)

Source: Compile from the Statistical Reports of Election Commission of India.

In Judicial system also, the women participation as judges is very marginal. In 2017, only 1 (out of 25) women judge is there in Supreme Court. In all the High Courts of the country, only 11 percent (74 females against 613 males) judges are females. The highest number of women judges are in the High Court of Bombay & Madras (11) followed by Delhi (10). Sikkim has the highest percentage share of female judges among its High Court Judges (33 percent, one female and two male judges).

Women Representation in Panchayati Raj Institutions

Women constitute half the world as well as in urban population. Despite their large numbers they have a very limited role to play in governance—policy and decision making as they are not sufficiently and properly represented in the local governments.. Though the functions and working of local bodies affect every man and woman, the latter has no or very minimal role as they are under-represented in leadership positions in local government institutions until recently. They do not have a role to influence local decisions resulting in insufficient access to services. This necessitates measures to provide equal representation in the municipal councils. As the local governments are closest to the community they are the best places to involve women in local policy and decision-making so as to enable them to contribute in the policies and decisions that impact provision of civic services and quality of life. Several factors including discrimination, family burdens, financial constraints to contest to local governments, cultural factors, etc., come in the way of women participation. The political empowerment requires transformation of existing political structures and processes that are more responsive to women.

As the World Declaration on Women in Local Governance, 1998 noted that the problems and challenges facing humanity are global but occur and have to be dealt with at the local level. Women have the equal right to freedom from poverty, discrimination and insecurity. To fight these problems and to meet the challenges of sustainable human development, it is critical that women are empowered and participated in local governments as decision-makers, planners and managers. The 73rd Constitution Amendment Act, 1992 for the first time widened the base to provide representation to hitherto under represented or unrepresented categories of the community, including women, in urban local self-government institutions. This has raised the question as to what key role women could play in urban governance. The 73rd Constitution Amendment Act, 1992 provided one-third reservation for women. Based on the experience gained over two decades, the Government of India proposed 50 percent reservation for women in urban local bodies. There are many programmes in the formal and informal sector which promoted women's participation in local development like urban basic services to poor (BSUP), SJSRY, self-help groups, Kudumbashree in Kerala, etc., with different degrees of success in mobilizing women and their participation in local planning and development. The reservation for women in the local bodies is aimed at securing their active involvement and support in socio-economic development. Reservations became very important as in the normal process women were reluctant to contest the elections either because of murkiness and violence that often characterize electoral politics (Prasad 2014).

The 73rd th Constitution Amendment Act, 1992 has laid foundations for the emergence of strong bottom up women leadership who could climb the ladder to occupy positions of power at the state and national levels. The 73rd Constitution Amendment Act, 1992 which provided a constitutional status for local governments in the country and considered a revolutionary and radical legislation, provided reservation of one-third of the strength of the council to women and also extended the same principle of reservation to women in other categories like SCs, STs apart from General category. The 73rd Constitution Amendment Act, 1992 entrusts, through the 11th Schedule, important development functions to panchayats which have a major bearing on the development of women and children. The ability of the local bodies to undertake these functions, particularly those relating to poverty alleviation, safeguarding the interests of the weaker sections would, to a great extent, depend on the composition of the members of the councils who influence the local decision-making process (Prasad 2014).

Role of Women in local Governance

Policy Role

Formulate development policies, prepare town development plans, take decisions regarding the integration of spatial development planning with economic development planning, lay down broad parameters for the future growth of the towns, mobilize resources to undertake both obligatory and discretionary functions, undertake measures for assisting the weaker sections, etc.

Development Role

Formulation, implementation and monitoring of development plans, including those for the weaker sections, women, etc. is their responsibility. Both national and state governments have articulated a number of development programmes. Formulation of city action plans under these schemes and ensuring their proper and effective implementation is a part of their development role. They have also to mobilize their share of the resources, to implement various plans and programmes wherever necessary.

Political Role

As peoples' representatives, the elected representatives are to be in constant touch with their constituents to reflect their aspirations, needs and perspectives in the articulation of town's development policies and plans. They are the links between the electors and the local body. Apart from this, as representatives of political parties they also have to undertake political activities. Sarpanches, Chairpersons and Members are constantly approached by their constituents with complaints or grievances relating to the functioning of panchayats . As people's responsibilities, they have to attend to their day-to-day problems and continuously establish rapport with the community.

Administrative Role

Supervising the functions of municipal officials in the implementation of development plans, monitoring their progress, ensuring the proper implementation of municipal laws and regulations, administrative coordination and convergence within the municipality and with external agencies, liasoning with non-governmental organizations, resolutions of conflicts in the management of municipal affairs between the groups and communities, effective utilization of resources both internal and external, etc. are some of their administrative roles. The Sarpanches and Chairpersons, who are directly elected and have a term co-terminus with that of the council, will tend to have more of these responsibilities.

In particular, women can play a purposive role as heads and members of councilors Panchayats (Prasad 2014):

- Ensuring access to basic services like water and sanitation and to provide higher allocation to these services. Enhancing the access of women to economic resources by strengthening linkages with banks and other financial institutions and encouraging innovative savings, thrift and lending practices.
- Ensuring access to education to all with a view to eradicate illiteracy, particularly among women and children.

- Improving access to women to vocational and technical training for skill formation and development.
- Increasing access to quality health care, particularly preventive and promotive health care, provision of information about factors which increase risks to women's health.
- Initiating measures for the prevention of violence against women, raising awareness among women on the issues of violence against women and organizing support to community-based organizations working in this field.
- Promoting women's economic right including access to employment and appropriate working conditions and strengthening women's economic capacity through skill development, training, self-employment and establishment of market and trade networks.
- Ensuring full participation of women at all levels of decision-making concerning the well-being of the society, particularly those concerning women, children and disadvantaged people.
- Preparing women to leadership positions, organizing legal and administrative literacy programmes to educate women on various aspects of their rights.
- Involving women's groups in environmental protection and up-gradation; and
- Protecting the rights of the children, particularly those of the girl child.

The 73rd and 74th Amendments (1992) to the Indian Constitution have served as a major breakthrough towards ensuring women's equal access and increased participation in political power structure. There are about one million elected women representatives in Panchayats and municipal bodies in India. The women representatives in ULBs of the selected states are shown in Table 6. It is estimated that elected women in all the three categories of ULBs account for 22622. However, a few states like Bihar, Madhya Pradesh and Rajasthan have declared to provide 50 percent reservation to women in ULBs elections. Thus, the number of elected women representatives is likely to increase. The 73rd and 74th Amendments (1992) to the Indian Constitution have served as a major breakthrough towards ensuring women's equal access and increased participation in political power structure. There are about one million elected women representatives in Panchayats and municipal bodies in India. The women representatives in ULBs of the selected states are shown in Table 3.4. It is estimated that elected women in all the three categories of ULBs account for 22622.

However, a few states like Bihar, Madhya Pradesh and Rajasthan have declared to provide 50 percent reservation to women in ULBs elections. Thus, the number of elected women representatives is likely to increase.

Table: 3.4 State wise Reservation of Women in Local Governments in India

S.No	*Name of the State*	*Reservation for women in Local Bodies*
1	Madhya Pradesh	50%
2	Chhattisgarh	50%
3	Manipur	33%
4	Bihar	50%
5	Rajasthan	50%
6	Odisha	50%
7	Uttar Pradesh	33%
8	Uttarakhand	33%
9	Jharkhand	50%
10	Sikkim	33%
11	Arunachal Pradesh	33%
12	Assam	50%
13	Nagaland	33%
14	Mizoram	33%
15	Tripura	50%
16	West Bengal	33%
17	Meghalaya	33%

Source: RCUES, Lucknow

The Constitutional Amendment Acts also ensured the provision of reservation of women in local governments. One-third seats were reserved in urban local bodies also. A few states such as Bihar, M.P., and Rajasthan have also made provision for 50 percent reservation for women in local governments. Thus the gender mainstreaming in decentralized governance has been initiated. More ever, women's share in policy perspective and resources allocation in urban sector has been reported to be very low. With the launch of JNNURM and other infrastructure programmes and schemes, gender mainstreaming is getting momentum. JNNURM and reforms agenda seek to improve the effectiveness, accountability, efficiency, sustainability and service equity in cities. It also aims to reduce class and gender fragmentation by making socio-political-economic institutions, processes and resource allocations more equitable. Thus, gender based urban development is about promoting cities that respond, equally to men and women. Urban women experience cities differently and thus meeting their needs becomes critical for promoting sustainable and equitable urban development (Singh, 2013).

The 73rd Amendment to the Indian Constitution, 1992 has served as a major breakthrough towards women's equal access and increased participation in local government. The Constitutional Amendment Act aims at constitutional guarantees to safeguard the interests of urban local government to enable them to function as effective and self governing institutions at grassroot level. This Amendment provides for reservation of 33 percent of elected seats for women at local government level in urban areas. There is also one-third reservation for women of posts of chairpersons for these local bodies. Involvement of women in the political arena and in decision making process is an important tool for empowerment as well as monitoring standards of political performance at local level. However, some of the major constraints prevent women from effective participation at local level.

In order to orient and provide training to women representatives in urban administration and municipal affairs, more than 60 organizations in India organize programmes for the capacity building of elected women representatives. Most of the organizations are working at the state level. Government of India under the Ministry of Urban Development provides financial support to the organizations and academic institutions for organizing training and orientation programmes for elected women representatives. However, 50 percent matching share was supposed to be mobilize from the concerned state. Now, Ministry has changed the norms and provides 100 percent funding to the organizations for conducting training programmes and orientation to the elected women representatives. Similarly, Ministry of Housing & Urban Poverty Alleviation, Govt. of India has also made provision to provide training and orientation to be elected representatives for orienting Urban Poverty Alleviation programmes in each state. There are a few institutions viz. AIILSG, NIUA, HSMI, SEWA, Working Women's Forum, YUVA, DISHA, PRAYAS, ASTHA, SNDT University, Aalochna, Agni, Stri Mukti Snagthan etc. emphasize on strengthening women's participation and women leadership. Besides Ministry of Urban Development, Government of India supports several training programmes being organized through Regional Centre for Urban & Environmental Studies located at Lucknow, New Delhi, Mumbai and Hyderabad. Department of Urban Development in various states have initiated several capacity building or training initiatives to train women working at various levels of municipal administration. National Academy of Administration, Mussourie is actively involved in training senior government officers from Public Service Commission. The Academy has also set up a National Centre for Gender Training and Research to further issues related to women and development. Ministry of Women and Child Development, Government of India in association with concerned state government is also organizing training, orientation programmes and workshops for the orientation on gender budgeting and gender sensitization. Ministry of Housing and Urban Poverty Alleviation, Government of India is also made provisions for 30 percent reservation in skill training, Urban Self Employment Programme, besides, exclusively Urban Women Self Help Programme under Revamped SJSRY. The revised Guidelines of SJSRY make provisions the there will be no project limit for financing the self employment projects while women will get subsidy upto Rs 300000 or 35 percent of the project under Urban Women Self Help Programme.

As per information available on March 1, 2013, women constituted 46.7 percent in Panchayati Raj Institutions in India. The proportion of women in Panchayats was reported high in the states of Jharkhand (58.6 percent), Uttarakhand (56.1 percent), Kerala (51.9 percent), Madhya Pradesh (50.5 percent), Himachal Pradesh (50.1 percent), Bihar (50 percent), Orissa (50 percent) and Sikkim (50 percent). Representation of women in Panchayati Raj Institution was reported low in Goa (32.3 percent), Andhra Pradesh (33.5 percent) and Gujarat (33 percent). It is to be noted that Bihar, Madhya Pradesh, Jharkhand, Chhattisgarh, Rajasthan, Himachal Pradesh, Kerala, Orissa, Uttarakhand and Sikkim have declared 50 per cent reservation for women in Panchayati Raj Institutions. Thus, the share of women in local governments is gradually increasing (Table 3.5). In 2016, at all India level 46 percent of the elected representatives in Panchayati Raj Institutions were women. The share of women elected members in Panchayati Raj institutions is highest in Jharkhand (59 percent) followed by Rajasthan (58 percent) and Uttarakhand (58 percent) and lowest in Daman & Diu (29 percent) followed by Arunachal Pradesh (33 percent), Goa (33 percent), Gujarat (33 percent) and Tamil Nadu (33 percent).

In view of the 73rd Constitution Amendment Act, the Haryana Panchayati Raj Act, 1994 was enacted with the provision of reservation of 1/3rd seats for women. At the time of fourth General Election, 2010, there were 6083 seats of Sarpanches and 58783 seats of Panches in 6083 Gram Panchayats, 2771 Members Panchayati Samiti in 119 Blocks and 374 Members of Zila Parishad in 21 districts.During 2013, 13.64 lakh women were found representing Panchayati Raj Institutions in India. Most of the women representatives in Panchayati Raj Institutions were reported from the states of Uttar Pradesh, Madhya Pradesh, Maharashtra, Chhattisgarh, Andhra Pradesh, Bihar, Rajasthan, Tamil Nadu and Gujarat. In the state of Haryana, 24876 women were found representing Panchayati Raj Institutions in all three tiers (Table 3.6).

Table: 3.5 State-wise Elected Women Representatives in Panchayats in India (As on March, 2013)

State	*Women*	*Total*	*per cent of Women*
Andhra Pradesh	85154	254487	33.5
Arunachal Pradesh	3889	9356	41.6
Assam	9903	26844	36.9
Bihar	68065	136130	50.0
Chhattisgarh	86538	158776	54.5
Goa	504	1559	32.3
Gujarat	39260	118751	33.0
Haryana	24786	68152	36.5
Himachal Pradesh	13947	27832	50.1
Jharkhand	31157	53207	58.6
Karnataka	41577	95307	43.6
Kerala	9907	1907	51.4
Madhya Pradesh	198459	393209	50.5
Maharashtra	101466	203203	49.9
Manipur	836	1723	48.5
Orissa	50431	100863	50.0
Punjab	29389	84138	34.9
Rajasthan	54673	109345	50.0
Sikkim	549	1099	50.0
Tamil Nadu	41790	119399	35.0
Tripura	2044	5676	36.0
Uttar Pradesh	309511	663980	40.0
Uttarakhand	34494	61452	56.1
West Bengal	19762	31423	28.4
All India	1364154	2921381	46.7

Source: Ministry of Panchayati Raj, Government of India.

Table: 3. 6 State-wise Elected Scheduled Castes, Scheduled Tribes and Women Representatives in Panchayats

States	*SC*	*ST*	*Women*	*Total*
Andhra Pradesh	46,755	21,078	85,154	254,487
Arunachal Pradesh	NA	9,356	3,889	9,356
Assam	1,344	886	9,903	26,844

(Contd...)

Bihar	22,201	1,053	68,065	136,130
Chhattisgarh	19,753	63,864	86,538	158,776
Goa	NA	92	504	1,559
Gujarat	8,340	23,719	39,206	118,751
Haryana	14,684	NA	24,876	68,152
Himachal Pradesh	7,467	1,215	13,947	27,832
Jammu & Kashmir	NA	NA	NA	NA
Jharkhand	5,870	18,136	31,157	53,207
Karnataka	17,723	10,275	41,577	95,307
Kerala	867	120	9,907	19,107
Madhya Pradesh	59,537	107,167	198,459	393,209
Maharashtra	22,175	30,211	101,466	203,203
Manipur	21	38	836	1,723
Odisha	16,390	22,240	NA	100,863
Punjab	26,937	NA	29,389	84,138
Rajasthan	18,807	13,777	54,673	109,345
Sikkim	77	418	NA	1,099
Tamil Nadu	28,655	1,194	41,790	119,399
Tripura	1,508	309	2,044	5,676
Uttar Pradesh	185,159	NA	309,511	773,980
Uttarakhand	12,230	2,067	34,494	61,452
West Bengal	17,605	4,168	19,762	51,423
All-India	568,181	342,157	1,364,154	2,921,381

Source: Ministry of Panchayati Raj, Government of India, 2013.

Representation of women in Panchayati Raj Institutions constituted 46.7 percent during 2013. In the state of Bihar, Jharkhand, Himachal Pradesh, Kerala, Madhya Pradesh, Maharashtra, Orissa, Rajasthan, Sikkim and Uttarakhand, representation of women was reported about 50 percent as many states have made provision for 50 percent reservation for women in PRIs and Local Governments. In the state of Haryana, women constituted 36.5 percent share in all Panchayati Raj Institutions (Table 3.7).

Table: 3.7 Proportion of Elected Scheduled Castes, Scheduled Tribes and Women Representatives in Panchayats

States	***SC***	***ST***	***Women***
Andhra Pradesh	18.4	8.3	33.5
Arunachal Pradesh	NA	100.0	41.6
Assam	5.0	3.3	36.9
Bihar	16.3	0.8	50.0
Chhattisgarh	12.4	40.2	54.5
Goa	NA	5.9	32.3
Gujarat	7.0	20.0	33.0

(*Contd...*)

Haryana	21.5	NA	36.5
Himachal Pradesh	26.8	4.4	50.1
Jammu & Kashmir	NA	NA	NA
Jharkhand	11.0	34.1	58.6
Karnataka	18.6	10.8	43.6
Kerala	4.5	0.6	51.9
Madhya Pradesh	15.1	27.3	50.5
Maharashtra	10.9	14.9	49.9
Manipur	1.2	2.2	48.5
Odisha	16.2	22.0	50.0
Punjab	32.0	NA	34.9
Rajasthan	17.2	12.6	50.0
Sikkim	7.0	38.0	50.0
Tamil Nadu	24.0	1.0	35.0
Tripura	26.6	5.4	36.0
Uttar Pradesh	23.9	NA	40.0
Uttarakhand	19.9	3.4	56.1
West Bengal	34.2	8.1	38.4
All-India	19.4	11.7	46.7

Source: Ministry of Panchayati Raj, Government of India, 2013.

Decentralization

Decentralization presents the opportunity for greater involvement of women in planning and consultation processes, and also has the potential for a more gender conscious allocation of local resources. Local authorities are closest to their citizens and hence in the best position to involve women in the decision-making process and in consultation. The decentralization of authority and resources is also an important means of improving stakeholder participation. However, struggles around resources at the local level can be unruly and local patron-client networks sometimes involve malfeasance and pork-barrel politics, which may serve further to exclude women rather than to encourage them into the political process. On the other hand the case of partnership in Mumbai cited above show how women's involvement may counter these trends.

Equity

Equity in the city implies representation as well as access to resources. Equity of access to decision-making and the basic necessities of urban life are basic to good urban governance. Yet there are countless ways in which income or social status affects people's ability to participate in city life and access its resources. Even when resources are available, public expenditure may be under-allocated in gender terms Women's rights to representation, as well as to basic services and other urban resources, cannot be denied.

Efficiency

The role women play in the urban economy is often not recognized because much of it takes place in the informal economy or hidden from view as home-working. Cities need to be efficient in terms of finances and administration. This means regulating and coordinating local authorities' management, and targeting finances for effective performance. In order to ensure this happens, women and men have to be able to contribute optimally to their own survival and the economy. A key challenge is to make visible and valued the contribution of women as well as men to the efficient operation of cities. Efficiency is compromised when women and the poor are not involved in decision-making and policy choices.

Transparency and Accountability

Studies demonstrate that the greater women's rights and the more women participate in public life, the less public sector corruption there is. However, women must be in a position to access, interpret and comment upon local government performance. Transparency and accountability depends upon city administrations and politics being open to public scrutiny. Communication needs to be accessible to people who cannot handle complex documents, to those not used to engaging in public debate, and to working parents with limited time — all factors affecting women more than men.

Civic Engagement and Citizenship

Governments and international agencies alike have increasingly appreciated the importance of women's grassroots organizations. The crucial role played by women organized on the ground — in advocating for services and providing infrastructure and basic services themselves in the absence of provision from other sources — cannot be over-emphasized. It is the responsibility of local authorities to encourage the full engagement of women citizens. It is also in their interests to do so to ensure the effective functioning of urban neighborhoods.

Security of Individuals and Their Environment

Insecure and even hostile urban environments can be perpetuated by local authorities' inattention to planning for women's security both domestically and in public places. Security of individuals and their environment is not confined to cities of the North or the South. It is a matter of growing urgency as unsafe cities restrict access and mobility for their citizens, especially women. Violence against women is just as likely to happen in the home as in public spaces. If women leave abusive relationships, they invariably lose their homes and security as well. Thus violence and the fear of violence prevent women from full and equal participation in the social life of their community and threaten our understanding of what should be the democratic functioning of our society. In recent years there has been a paradigm shift from urban governance to good urban governance underpinning sustainability, decentralization, equity, efficiency, transparency and accountability, civic engagement and security. Though the role and contributions of local representatives to achieve good urban governance (GUG) is common to both men and women, there are specific gender aspects that should be understood, as can be seen from the Table given below (Khosla, 2009).

Political empowerment of women is gaining importance in the era of decentralized governance. Women are actively participating in decision making process and functioning of Panchayati Raj Institutions. The reservation for women in local governments has been increased upto 50 per cent in many states in view of the growing importance of gender equality and women empowerment. Over the period, there has been increasing share of women in Panchayati Raj Institutions in various states. Women from Backward communities and weaker sections are also coming forward in Panchayat elections.

Chapter - 4

Profile of Respondents

Political empowerment of women is imperative to ensure engendering development and gender equality in development planning. Women's participation in decision making process is essential for political empowerment. Panchayati Raj Institutions are playing critical role in political empowerment of women. These institutions are creating greater opportunities for women in decision making process at the grass root level. The decentralization process and implementation of 73rd Constitution Amendment Act has provided 1/3rd reservation for women in Panchayati Raj Institutions. Some of the states have also enhanced the quota of reservation up to 50 percent for women in Panchayati Raj Institutions and Urban Local Governments. Elected women in Panchayati raj Institutions are actively involved in decision making process besides their participation in planning and implementation of development programmes and schemes. In this part of the dissertation, an attempt has been made to examine the socio-economic profile of the elected women as Sarpanch from selected districts of Haryana and Gujarat.

Age of respondents is shown in Table 4.1. Most of the respondents were found belonging to the age group of less than 50 years while about 18 percent respondents were from the age group of above 50 years. Respondents from lower age group were recorded high in Gujarat while respondents from higher age group were recorded high in Haryana.

Table: 4.1 Age of Respondents

State	*20-30 Years*	*31-40 Years*	*41-50 Years*	*51-60 Years*	*61-70 Years*	*71-80 Years*	*81-90 Years*	*Total*
Gujarat	22	107	139	22	6	0	0	296
	7.4%	36.1%	47.0%	7.4%	2.0%	0.0%	0.0%	100.0%
Haryana	27	107	83	44	34	4	1	300
	9.0%	35.7%	27.7%	14.7%	11.3%	1.3%	0.3%	100.0%

(Contd...)

Haryana	27	107	83	44	34	4	1	300
	9.0%	35.7%	27.7%	14.7%	11.3%	1.3%	0.3%	100.0%

Source: Field Survey

Category of respondents is shown in Table 4.2. More than half of the respondents were from General category. This was found more pronouncing in Haryana (55 per cent) as compared to Gujarat (48.3 per cent). About 22 per cent respondents in Haryana were OBCs while about 45 percent respondents in Gujarat were Scheduled Caste/Scheduled Tribes.

Table: 4.2 Category of Respondents

State	*General*	*OBC*	*SC/ST*	*Total*
Gujarat	143	20	133	296
	48.3%	6.8%	44.9%	100.0%
Haryana	165	67	68	300
	55.0%	22.3%	22.7%	100.0%
Total	308	87	201	596
	51.7%	14.6%	33.7%	100.0%

Source: Field Survey

Religion of respondents is shown in Table 4.3. Most of the respondents were Hindus however, a significant proportion of respondents in Haryana were Sikhs. A negligible proportion of respondents in Gujarat were Muslims.

Table: 4.3 Religion of Respondents

State	*Hindu*	*Muslim*	*Sikh*	*Total*
Gujarat	294	2	0	296
	99.3%	0.7%	0.0%	100.0%
Haryana	284	0	16	300
	94.7%	0.0%	5.3%	100.0%
Total	578	2	16	596
	97.0%	0.3%	2.7%	100.0%

Source: Field Survey

Marital status of respondents is shown in Table 4.4. Most of the respondents were found married. This was found more pronouncing in Haryana (95.3 percent). A significant proportion of respondents in Gujarat were unmarried (8.8 percent). Similarly, about 4 per cent respondents in Haryana were widows.

Education of respondents is shown in Table 4.5. About 1/3rd respondents were primary pass. This was found more pronouncing in Gujarat (44.3 percent). About 22 percent respondents were middle pass while about 16 percent respondents were matric pass. The proportion of matric pass respondents was recorded high in Haryana (23 percent) while middle pass respondents was recorded high in Gujarat (30.1 percent). About 11 percent respondents were graduates and post graduates. This was found more pronouncing in Gujarat (13.5 percent) as against Haryana (8.4 percent). About 30 per cent respondents in Haryana were illiterate.

Table: 4.4 Marital Status of Respondents

State	*Married*	*Unmarried*	*Divorcee*	*Widow*	*Total*
Gujarat	268	26	2	0	296
	90.5%	8.8%	0.7%	0.0%	100.0%
Haryana	286	1	0	13	300
	95.3%	0.3%	0.0%	4.3%	100.0%
Total	554	27	2	13	596
	93.0%	4.5%	0.3%	2.2%	100.0%

Source: Field Survey

Table: 4.5 Education of Respondents

State	*Primary*	*Middle*	*Matric*	*Graduate*	*Other*	*Illiterate*	*P.G*	*Total*
Gujarat	131	89	27	32	4	5	8	296
	44.3%	30.1%	9.1%	10.8%	1.4%	1.7%	2.7%	100.0%
Haryana	68	44	69	14	3	91	11	300
	22.7%	14.7%	23.0%	4.7%	1.0%	30.3%	3.7%	100.0%
Total	199	133	96	46	7	96	19	596
	33.4%	22.3%	16.1%	7.7%	1.2%	16.1%	3.2%	100.0%

Source: Field Survey.

Schooling of girl children is shown in Table 4.6. About 1/4th respondents reported that girl children are enrolled in girl schools. This was found more pronouncing in Haryana (34.3 percent). About 3/4th respondents revealed that girl children are getting education from co-education institutions. This was found more pronouncing in Gujarat (84.8 percent).

Table: 4.6 Schooling of Girl Children

State	*Girls*	*Co-Education*	*Total*
Gujarat	45	251	296
	15.2%	84.8%	100.0%
Haryana	103	197	300
	34.3%	65.7%	100.0%
Total	148	448	596
	24.8%	75.2%	100.0%

Source: Field Survey

Age at the time of marriage is shown in Table 4.7. About 3/4th respondents reported that they were married at the age of 16-20 years. It was found more pronouncing in Haryana (77.3 percent). About 5 per cent respondents in Haryana revealed that they were married at the age of 10-15 years. About 21 percent respondents further reported that they were married at the age of 20-25 years. It was found more pronouncing in Gujarat (25.3 percent). A higher proportion of respondents in Haryana were married at the lower age while in Gujarat a higher proportion of respondents were married in middle age group.

Table: 4.7 Age At The Time of Marriage

State	*10-15 Years*	*16-20 Years*	*21-25 Years*	*26-30 Years*	*36-40 Years*	*Total*
Gujarat	4	207	75	10	0	296
	1.4%	69.9%	25.3%	3.4%	0.0%	100.0%
Haryana	16	232	48	3	1	300
	5.3%	77.3%	16.0%	1.0%	0.3%	100.0%
Total	20	439	123	13	1	596
	3.4%	73.7%	20.6%	2.2%	0.2%	100.0%

Source: Field Survey

Type of family of respondents is shown in Table 4.8. More than 3/4th respondents were from joint families. This was found more pronouncing in Gujarat (77.7 percent). Similarly, more than 1/4th respondents in Haryana were from nuclear families.

Table: 4.8 Type of Family of Respondents

State	*Joint*	*Nuclear*	*Total*
Gujarat	230	66	296
	77.7%	22.3%	100.0%
Haryana	222	78	300
	74.0%	26.0%	100.0%
Total	452	144	596
	75.8%	24.2%	100.0%

Source: Field Survey

Family occupation of respondents is shown in Table 4.9. Majority of the respondents reported that their main family occupation is agriculture. This was found more pronouncing in Haryana (76 percent). Less than 1/4th respondents in Gujarat were labours while about 21 percent respondents in Gujarat were in private and government service. A significant proportion of respondents in Haryana reported that their family occupation is business.

Table: 4.9 Family Occupation of Respondents

State		*Agriculture*	*Animal Husbandry*	*Business*	*Govt. Service*	*Job*	*Labour*	*Private Service*	*Total*
Gujarat		143	8	14	4	4	68	55	296
		48.3%	2.7%	4.7%	1.4%	1.4%	23.0%	18.6%	100.0%
Haryana		228	0	13	5	0	38	16	300
		76.0%	0.0%	4.3%	1.7%	0.0%	12.7%	5.3%	100.0%
Total		371	8	27	9	4	106	71	596
		62.2%	1.3%	4.5%	1.5%	0.7%	17.8%	11.9%	100.0%

Source: Field Survey

Profession of respondents is shown in Table 4.10. About 63 percent respondents reported that they are housewives. This was found more pronouncing in Haryana (80.7 percent). About 23 percent respondents in Gujarat were in service while about 17 percent respondents in Haryana were cultivators and labours.

Table: 4.10 Profession of Respondents

State	*Cultivator*	*Labour*	*Service*	*Housewife*	*Others*	*Total*
Gujarat	49	35	67	131	14	296
	16.6%	11.8%	22.6%	44.3%	4.7%	100.0%
Haryana	43	10	1	242	4	300
	14.3%	3.3%	0.3%	80.7%	1.3%	100.0%
Total	92	45	68	373	18	596
	15.4%	7.6%	11.4%	62.6%	3.0%	100.0%

Source: Field Survey

Husband's profession of respondents is shown in Table 4.11. More than half of the respondents revealed that the profession of their spouse is agriculture. This was found more pronouncing in Haryana (62.7 percent). About 17 percent respondents reported that their husbands are in private service. This was found more pronouncing in Gujarat (25.3 percent). About 15 percent respondents further reported that their husbands are labours. This was found more pronouncing in Gujarat (18. 9 percent).

Monthly family income from different sources is shown in Table 4.12. More than half of the respondents reported that their monthly family income is less than ₹ 10,000. This was found more pronouncing in Gujarat (72 percent). About 30 per cent respondents further reported that their monthly family income is in between ₹ 10,000 to ₹ 30,000. This was found more pronouncing in Haryana (43.6 percent). Thus, about 16 per cent respondents revealed that their monthly family income is more than ₹ 30,000.

Table: 4.11 Husband's Profession of Respondents

State		Agriculture	Animal Husbandry	Business	Expired	Govt. Service	Head Master/ Teacher	Labour	Not Applicable	Other	Private Service	Retired	Total
Gujarat		117	2	20	0	0	0	56	26	0	75	0	296
		39.5%	0.7%	6.8%	0.0%	0.0%	0.0%	18.9%	8.8%	0.0%	25.3%	0.0%	100.0%
Haryana		188	0	18	1	8	3	32	14	2	26	8	300
		62.7%	0.0%	6.0%	0.3%	2.7%	1.0%	10.7%	4.7%	0.7%	8.7%	2.7%	100.0%
Total		305	2	38	1	8	3	88	40	2	101	8	596
		51.2%	0.3%	6.4%	0.2%	1.3%	0.5%	14.8%	6.7%	0.3%	16.9%	1.3%	100.0%

Source: Field Survey

Table: 4.12 Monthly Family Income From Different Sources

State	*Less Than Rs. 5000*	*Rs.6000-Rs.10000*	*Rs.11000-Rs.20000*	*Rs.21000-Rs.30000*	*Rs.31000-Rs.40000*	*Rs.41000 Rs.50000*	*More Than Rs.51000*	*Total*
Gujarat	169	44	17	29	25	12	0	296
	57.1%	14.9%	5.7%	9.8%	8.4%	4.1%	0.0%	100.0%
Haryana	44	65	88	43	14	19	27	300
	14.7%	21.7%	29.3%	14.3%	4.7%	6.3%	9.0%	100.0%
Total	213	109	105	72	39	31	27	596
	35.7%	18.3%	17.6%	12.1%	6.5%	5.2%	4.5%	100.0%

Source: Field Survey

Land holding of family is shown in Table 4.13. More than 2/5th respondents revealed that they are landless. This was found more pronouncing in Gujarat (58.4 per cent). About 2/5th respondents in Haryana further revealed that their land holdings are less than 5 acres. About 1/4th respondents in Haryana reported that their land holdings are in between 6 to 30 acres. The size of landholdings was recorded high in Haryana as compared to Gujarat.

Table: 4.13 Land Holding of Family

State	*Less Than 5*	*6-10*	*11-20*	*21-30*	*31-40*	*41-50*	*51-60*	*More Than 60*	*None*	*Total*
Gujarat	83	16	20	0	2	0	0	2	173	296
	28.0%	5.4%	6.8%	0.0%	0.7%	0.0%	0.0%	0.7%	58.4%	100.0%
Haryana	119	60	28	17	2	1	1	0	72	300
	39.7%	20.0%	9.3%	5.7%	0.7%	0.3%	0.3%	0.0%	24.0%	100.0%
Total	202	76	48	17	4	1	1	2	245	596
	33.9%	12.8%	8.1%	2.9%	0.7%	0.2%	0.2%	0.3%	41.1%	100.0%

Source: Field Survey

Experience in active politics is shown in Table 4.14. Most of the respondents revealed that their experience in active politics is less than 5 years. However, about 15 percent respondents in Gujarat reported that they have more than 5 years political experience.

Table: 4.14 Experience in Active Politics in Years

State	*1*	*2*	*3*	*4*	*5*	*7*	*9*	*10*	*20*	*25*	*Total*
Gujarat	83	24	16	19	10	2	0	18	4	4	180
	46.1%	13.3%	8.9%	10.6%	5.6%	1.1%	0.0%	10.0%	2.2%	2.2%	100.0%
Haryana	32	1	4	76	5	1	2	2	1	0	124
	25.8%	0.8%	3.2%	61.3%	4.0%	0.8%	1.6%	1.6%	0.8%	0.0%	100.0%
Total	115	25	20	95	15	3	2	20	5	4	304
	37.8%	8.2%	6.6%	31.2%	4.9%	1.0%	0.7%	6.6%	1.6%	1.3%	100.0%

Source: Field Survey

The respondents were asked that whether they are member of any political party. Less than 2/4th respondents reported that they are members of political parties. This was found more pronouncing in Gujarat (55.4 percent). Thus, more than 3/4th respondents in Haryana were not associated with political party.

Table: 4.15 Are You A Member of Any Political Party

State	*Yes*	*No*	*Total*
Gujarat	164	132	296
	55.4%	44.6%	100.0%
Haryana	66	234	300
	22.0%	78.0%	100.0%
Total	230	366	596
	38.6%	61.4%	100.0%

Source: Field Survey

The respondents were further asked that whether their election was influenced by family members. Most of the respondents revealed that their election was influenced by their family members mainly their husbands. It was found more pronouncing in Haryana (82.7 percent). A large proportion of respondents in Gujarat further reported that their election was influenced by their fathers and political parties (Table 4.16).

The respondents were asked that who were responsible for arousal in them were. Majority of the respondents reported that their family and relatives were main agents responsible for their arousal. This was found more pronouncing in Haryana. Political and social workers were also found responsible for arousal in political representatives in Gujarat (Table 4.17).

Table: 4.16 Whether Your Elections is Influenced By Family Members

State	*Father*	*Husband*	*Party*	*Any Other*	*Total*
Gujarat	26	208	24	38	296
	8.8%	70.3%	8.1%	12.8%	100.0%
Haryana	10	248	2	40	300
	3.3%	82.7%	0.7%	13.3%	100.0%
Total	36	456	26	78	596
	6.0%	76.5%	4.4%	13.1%	100.0%

Source: Field Survey

Table: 4.17 Who Were Responsible For Arousal in You

State	*Family/ Relatives*	*School/ College*	*Political And Social Workers*	*Newspapers And Books*	*Caste Affinity*	*Total*
Gujarat	195	2	83	12	4	296
	65.9%	0.7%	28.0%	4.1%	1.4%	100.0%
Haryana	268	1	22	4	5	300
	89.3%	0.3%	7.3%	1.3%	1.7%	100.0%
Total	463	3	105	16	9	596
	77.7%	0.5%	17.6%	2.7%	1.5%	100.0%

Source: Field Survey

The profile of women Sarpanchs in Panchayati Raj Institutions of simply demonstrates that they are mainly from the middle age group. More than half of the elected women are from the General Caste. However, their educational level is found to be poor. They mainly belong to joint families. The main family occupation is predominantly agriculture and petty business. Their monthly family income is also reported to be less. Most of the women were elected for the first time and thus, their experience in active politics is either low or nil. Only a small proportion of respondents were found affiliated with political parties. Family support in the arousal of women Sarpanchs has been reported to be higher.

Chapter - 5

Role and Responsibilities of Woman Sarpanchs

Political participation of women is an important aspect of engendering development and women empowerment. The decentralized governance has created opportunities for women to take active participation in decision making process and implementation of rural development programmes in India. Women's engagement in development planning and implementation of programmes and schemes has wider implications on governance and development of the region. In this part of the dissertation, an attempt has been made to examine the profile of women heads of Village Panchayats and their participation in decision making process and development planning.

The respondents were asked that whether they were elected for the first time. About 87 per cent respondents revealed that they were elected for the first time. It was found more pronouncing in the state of Haryana (97.3 percent) as compared to Gujarat (77 percent) (Table 5.1).

Table: 5.1 Whether Elected First Time

State	*Yes*	*No*	*Total*
Gujarat	228	68	296
	77.0%	23.0%	100.0%
Haryana	292	8	300
	97.3%	2.7%	100.0%
Total	520	76	596
	87.2%	12.8%	100.0%

Source: Field Survey.

Those who were elected for second or more times, were mainly higher and same positions earlier. However, a higher proportion of respondents in Gujarat were elected for second or more times (Table 5.2).

Table: 5.2 Earlier Position Held by Women

State		Same	Higher	Lower	Not Applicable	Total
Gujarat		16	30	22	226	296
		5.4%	10.1%	7.4%	76.4%	100.0%
Haryana		6	1	1	292	300
		2.0%	0.3%	0.3%	97.3%	100.0%
Total		22	31	23	518	596
		3.7%	5.2%	3.8%	86.9%	100.0%

Source: Field Survey

Terms as Sarpanch are shown in Table 5.3. About 87 percent respondents were elected for the first time while about 5 per cent respondents were elected as Sarpanch as second term. Thus, about 8 percent respondents revealed that they were elected third or more than 3 times.

Table: 5.3 Terms As Sarpanch

State	1st	2nd	3rd	More Than 3	Total
Gujarat	228	28	20	20	296
	77.0%	9.5%	6.8%	6.8%	100.0%
Haryana	292	1	5	2	300
	97.3%	0.3%	1.7%	0.7%	100.0%
Total	520	29	25	20	596
	87.2%	4.9%	4.2%	3.7%	100.0%

Source: Field Survey

The respondents were asked that whether they elected as reserved candidates. About 1/3rd candidates revealed that they were elected as General candidates. This was found more pronouncing in Gujarat as compared to Haryana (Table 5.4).

Table: 5.4 Whether Elected As Reserved Candidate

State	General	Reserved	Total
Gujarat	106	190	296
	35.8%	64.2%	100.0%
Haryana	85	215	300
	28.3%	71.7%	100.0%
Total	191	405	596
	32.0%	68.0%	100.0%

Source: Field Survey

Type of reservation is shown in Table 5.5. About 63 percent respondents reported that they were elected against the seat reserved women candidates. It was found more pronouncing in Gujarat (67.9 percent). About 30 percent respondents in Haryana reported that they were elected against the seats reserved for Scheduled Caste women.

Table: 5.5 Type of Reservation

State		*For Woman*	*For BC*	*For SC*	*Total*
Gujarat		129	33	28	190
		67.9%	17.4%	14.7%	100.0%
Haryana		125	26	64	215
		58.1%	12.1%	29.8%	100.0%
Total		254	59	92	405
		62.7%	14.6%	22.7%	100.0%

Source: Field Survey

The respondents were asked that whether gram panchayat has constituted sub committees at gram panchayat level. In view of promoting decentralized rural governance, committees on education, health and sanitation, agriculture, housing, social justice etc. are being constituted at village panchayat level. Elected members of village panchayat are also elected in these committees for their effective role in rural development. About 82 percent respondents revealed that committees at village panchayat level have been constituted. It was found more pronouncing in Gujarat (88.5 percent) as compared to Haryana (76.3 percent). However, a large proportion of respondents in Haryana were not aware about such committees (Table 5.6).

Table: 5.6 Whether Gram Panchayat Has Constituted Sub Committees At Gram Panchayat Level

State	*Yes*	*No*	*Don't Know*	*Total*
Gujarat	262	28	6	296
	88.5%	9.5%	2.0%	100.0%
Haryana	229	19	52	300
	76.3%	6.3%	17.3%	100.0%
Total	491	47	58	596
	82.4%	7.9%	9.7%	100.0%

Source: Field Survey

The awareness about rural development schemes are shown in Table 5.7. Awareness about widow pension scheme, Indira awas yojana, old age pension scheme, Ladali scheme and MGNREGA was reported high. However, awareness about rural development schemes varies across the selected states.

Average strength during meeting of Gram Sabha is shown in Table 5.8. Slightly more than'1/4th respondents revealed that all members present during the meetings of Gram Sabha. This was found more pronouncing in Gujarat (44.6 percent). Similarly, more than 1/4th respondents further reported that 36-70 percent members are generally attend meetings of Gram

Sabha. It was found more pronouncing in Haryana (50 percent). About 1/3rd respondents in Gujarat reported that more than 70 percent members are attending the meetings of Gram Sabha.

Table: 5.7 Awareness About Rural Development Schemes

	Gujarat	*Haryana*	*Total*
Old Age Pension	84	291	375
	28.4%	97.0%	62.9%
MGNREGA	211	140	351
	71.3%	46.7%	58.9%
National Rural Livelihood Mission	74	133	207
	25.0%	44.3%	34.7%
Indira Awaas yojna	159	249	408
	53.7%	83.0%	68.5%
Total Sanitation Campaign	133	168	301
	44.9%	56.0%	50.5%
District Plan	100	131	231
	33.8%	43.7%	38.8%
14th Finance Commission	175	99	274
	59.1%	33.0%	46.0%
State Rural Development Fund	95	150	245
	32.1%	50.0%	41.1%
Member Of Parliament Local Area Development Scheme	103	118	221
	34.8%	39.3%	37.1%
Widow Pension	170	288	458
	57.4%	96.0%	76.8%
Ladli Scheme	102	267	369
	34.5%	89.0%	61.9%
Any other	16	29	45
	5.4%	9.7%	7.6%

Source: Field Survey

Table: 5.8 Average Strength During Meeting of Gram Sabha

State	*10 -19 % Presented*	*20- 35 % Presented*	*36-70 % Presented*	*71- 90 % Presented*	*Half Member Are Presented*	*Yes All Member Presented*	*Total*
Gujarat	28	6	12	96	22	132	296
	9.5%	2.0%	4.1%	32.4%	7.4%	44.6%	100.0%
Haryana	15	60	150	31	17	27	300
	5.0%	20.0%	50.0%	10.3%	5.7%	9.0%	100.0%
Total	43	66	162	127	39	159	596
	7.2%	11.1%	27.2%	21.3%	6.5%	26.7%	100.0%

Source: Field Survey

The respondents were asked that whether women members are attending the meetings of the Gram Sabha. Most of the respondents revealed that women members are attending Gram Sabha meetings. However, about 6 percent respondents in Haryana revealed that women members are not attending Gram Sabha meetings (Table 5.9).

Table: 5.9 Whether Women of The Community Attend The Gram Sabha Meetings

State	*Yes*	*No*	*Total*
Gujarat	292	4	296
	98.6%	1.4%	100.0%
Haryana	282	18	300
	94.0%	6.0%	100.0%
Total	574	22	596
	96.3%	3.7%	100.0%

Source: Field Survey

Methods for information about the meetings of Gram Sabha are shown in Table 5.10. Informal communication in Haryana and notice in Gujarat was reported the main source of information regarding the meetings of Gram Sabha. Similarly, informal communication such as messenger, through members and through children in Haryana were found more popular while in Gujarat agenda by signature was found more popular as a means to communicate members of community regarding meetings of Gram Sabha.

Table: 5.10 Method For Information About Meetings of Gram Sabha

State	*Advertisement*	*Agenda By Signature*	*By Children*	*Choukidar*	*Meeting*	*Message Through Mobile Phone*	*Munaadi*	*Munadi*	*Notice*	*Through Panchs*	*Total*
Gujarat	14	60	0	0	0	0	0	14	194	14	296
	4.7%	20.3%	0.0%	0.0%	0.0%	0.0%	0.0%	4.7%	65.5%	4.7%	100.0%
Haryana	0	3	14	74	6	16	1	178	1	7	300
	0.0%	1.0%	4.7%	24.7%	2.0%	5.3%	0.3%	59.3%	0.3%	2.3%	100.0%
Total	14	63	14	74	6	16	1	192	195	21	596
	2.3%	10.6%	2.3%	12.4%	1.0%	2.7%	0.2%	32.2%	32.7%	3.5%	100.0%

Source: Field Survey

Methods being adopted in identification of beneficiaries in various schemes are shown in Table 5.11. Serving notice, communication approaching through members and direct approach to beneficiaries are some of the major methods being adopted for identification of beneficiaries in various schemes. However, methods for identification of beneficiaries in various schemes vary across the selected states.

Table: 5.11 Method being adopted in identification of Beneficiaries in Various Schemes

	Gujarat	*Haryana*	*Total*
Serve Notice	187	80	267
	63.2%	26.7%	44.8%
Through Panches	25	162	187
	8.4%	54.0%	31.4%
Political Influence	4	15	19
	1.4%	5.0%	3.2%
Direct Approach To Beneficiary	7	39	46
	2.4%	13.0%	7.7%
Any other	160	146	306
	54.1%	48.7%	51.3%

Source: Field Survey

Methods being adopted for passing of resolution are shown in Table 5.12. About 81 per cent respondents revealed that resolutions are being passed in Gram Sabha meetings. It was found more pronouncing in Haryana (87 percent) as compared to Gujarat (74.7 percent). About 19 percent respondents in Gujarat revealed that resolutions are being passed through door to door signature campaign.

Table: 5.12 Methods Being Adopted for Passing of Resolution

State	*In Gram Sabha Meeting*	*Through Voting*	*Door To Door For Signature*	*Any Other*	*Total*
Gujarat	221	19	56	0	296
	74.7%	6.4%	18.9%	0.0%	100.0%
Haryana	261	17	16	6	300
	87.0%	5.7%	5.3%	2.0%	100.0%
Total	482	36	72	6	596
	80.9%	6.0%	12.1%	1.0%	100.0%

Source: Field Survey

Development of agriculture including agriculture extension is shown in Table 5.13. Less than 2/5th respondents reported that development of waste land is being ensured under their leadership. It was found more pronouncing in Haryana (57.7 percent) as compared to Gujarat (18.6 percent). About 30 percent respondents further reported that distribution of improved seeds, manure and fertilizers is being ensured under their supervision. It was found more pronouncing in Haryana as compared to Gujarat.

Table: 5.13 Development of Agriculture Including Agriculture Extension

	Gujarat	*Haryana*	*Total*
Preventing There Unauthorized Alienation And Use	32	71	103
	10.8%	23.7%	17.3%
Recover The Loan Amount Up Keep Of Accounts And Records	38	71	109
	12.8%	23.7%	18.3%
Development Of Waste Lands	55	173	228
	18.6%	57.7%	38.3%
Distribution Of Improved Seeds Manure And Fertilizers	68	110	178
	23.0%	36.7%	29.9%

Source: Field Survey

Minor irrigation, water management and watershed development are shown in Table 5.14. Majority of the respondents reported that they assist in development of ground water resources. It was found more pronouncing in Gujarat (80.1 percent) as compared to Haryana (57.3 percent). About 50 percent respondents in Haryana reported that they identify the sites for construction of minor irrigation. However, majority of respondents revealed that they are not involved in selection of sites for minor irrigation. Similarly, about 31 percent respondents reported that they are not involved in development of ground water resources.

Table: 5.14 Minor Irrigation Water Management and Watershed Development

	Gujarat	*Haryana*	*Total*
Identify The Sites For The Construction Of Minor Irrigation	73	150	223
	24.7%	50.0%	37.4%
Assist In Development Of Ground Water Resources	237	172	409
	80.1%	57.3%	68.6%

Source: Field Survey

Development of social forestry and farm forestry is shown in Table 5.15. The overwhelming majority of respondents revealed that they are involved in development of social forestry and conservation of forest. This was found more pronouncing in Gujarat (82.8 percent) as compared to Haryana (76.7 percent). However, a significant proportion of respondents revealed that they are not involved in development of social forestry and its conservation.

Development of rural housing is shown in Table 5.16. About 3/4th respondents revealed that they are active in implementation of Indira Awas Yojana while about 1/3rd respondents were found active in implementation of Pradhan Mantri Gramoydaya Yojana and Renovation/ repairing of housing belonging to Scheduled Caste and Scheduled Tribes. About 1/4th respondents further reported that they are active in monitoring of rural housing scheme and submitting quarterly report to the concerned department. However, involvement of elected representatives in implementation of rural housing schemes varies across the selected states.

Table: 5.15 Development of Social Forestry and Farm Forestry

State	*Plantation And Preservation Of Trees On The Sides Of Roads And Other Public Lands Under Its Control*	*Any Other*	*No*	*Total*
Gujarat	245	37	14	296
	82.8%	12.5%	4.7%	100.0%
Haryana	230	38	32	300
	76.7%	12.7%	10.7%	100.0%
Total	475	75	46	596
	79.7%	12.6%	7.7%	100.0%

Source: Field Survey

Table: 5.16 Development of Rural Housing

	Gujarat	*Haryana*	*Total*
Monitoring The Scheme And Submit A Quarterly Report To Zilaparishad/Parent Department	16	131	147
	5.4%	43.7%	24.7%
Renovation / Repairing Of Housing Belonging To SC/ST	51	158	209
	17.2%	52.7%	35.1%
Implementation Of Indira Awaas Yojna	225	219	444
	76.0%	73.0%	74.5%
Implementation Of Pradhan Mantra Gramodaya Yojana (Awas) PMGY	88	93	181
	29.7%	31.0%	30.4%

Source: Field Survey

Provision of drinking water is shown in Table 5.17. Majority of the respondents reported that they are involved in promotion of drinking water and rural sanitation programme. This was found more pronouncing in Gujarat as compared to Haryana. About 64 percent respondents further reported that they are active in maintenance of rural water supply scheme. It was found more pronouncing in Gujarat (67.6 percent) as compared to Haryana (60.7 percent). Majority of the respondents in Haryana reported that they are active in construction, repair and maintenance of drinking water wells, tanks and ponds.

Development of rural electrification is shown in Table 5.18. About 3/4th respondents reported that they are involved in maintenance of street lighting while about 86 per cent respondents were found active in provision and maintenance of lighting of public streets and other places. However, it was recorded significantly high in Gujarat as compared to Haryana.

Table: 5.17 Provision of Drinking Water

	Gujarat	*Haryana*	*Total*
Promotion Of Drinking Water And Rural Sanitation Programme	234	200	434
	79.1%	66.7%	72.8%
Construction, Repairs And Maintenance Of Drinking Water Wells, Tanks And Ponds	132	213	345
	44.6%	71.0%	57.9%
Maintenance Of Rural Water Supply Scheme	200	182	382
	67.6%	60.7%	64.1%
Deepening Or Otherwise Improve Any Watercourse And Other Property	54	77	131
	18.2%	25.7%	22.0%

Source: Field Survey

Table: 5.18 Development of Rural Electrification

	Gujarat	*Haryana*	*Total*
Providing And Maintenance Of Lighting Of Public Streets And Other Places	276	237	513
	93.2%	79.0%	86.1%
Maintenance Of Street Lights	211	228	439
	71.3%	76.0%	73.7%

Source: Field Survey

Poverty alleviation programmes are shown in Table 5.19. Active role of elected representatives in poverty alleviation programmes was not found significant as majority of the respondents revealed that they are not involved in implementation of poverty alleviation programmes. However, less than half of the respondents in Haryana revealed that they are involved in disbursement of payment to beneficiaries and monitoring the poverty alleviation schemes and submitting quarterly reports to District Panchayat.

Table: 5.19 Poverty Alleviation Programme

	Gujarat	*Haryana*	*Total*
Disburse The Payment	14	144	158
	4.7%	48.0%	26.5%
Engage In Recovery If Any	42	64	106
	14.2%	21.3%	17.8%

(Contd...)

Monitor The Schemes And Submit Quarterly Report To District Panchayat	72	144	216
	24.3%	48.0%	36.2%

Source: Field Survey

Development of education is shown in Table 5.20. Majority of the respondents reported that they are ensuring enrolment and attendance in primary schools, supervising construction, repairs and maintenance of primary school buildings with help of Work Committee, monitoring Mid-Day Meal Scheme through Education Committee and monitoring enrolment and dropout in primary and secondary schools.

Table: 5.20 Development of Education

	Gujarat	*Haryana*	*Total*
Monitor Enrolment And Dropout Rates From I To Viii Std.	223	144	367
	75.3%	48.0%	61.6%
Public Awareness And Participation In Primary And Secondary Education	123	205	328
	41.6%	68.3%	55.0%
Supervise Construction, Repairs And Maintenance Of Primary School Building With Help To Work Committee	193	182	375
	65.2%	60.7%	62.9%
Education Committee Will Monitor The Mid Day Meal Scheme And Send A Report To The District Panchayat	184	218	402
	62.2%	72.7%	67.4%
Ensuring Full Enrolment And Attendance In Primary Schools	220	180	400
	74.3%	60.0%	67.1%

Source: Field Survey

Development of health and sanitation is shown in Table 5.21. More than half of the respondents reported that they are involved in promotion of health awareness and identification of sites for construction of public / community toilets. About 59 percent respondents revealed that they are involved in management of waste water and sewerage. It was found more pronouncing in Gujarat as compared to Haryana. More than 2/5th respondents further reported that they are involved in maintenance of public toilets.

Women and child development schemes are shown in Table 5.22. Majority of the respondents reported that they are participating in the implementation of women and child welfare programmes. It was found more pronouncing in Gujarat (87.5 percent) as compared to Haryana

(74.7 percent). Majority of the respondents further reported that they are involved in promotion of health and nutrition programmes.

Table: 5.21 Development of Health and Sanitation

	Gujarat	*Haryana*	*Total*
Identify Sites For Construction Of Public Latrines	164	148	312
	55.4%	49.3%	52.3%
Maintenance Of Public Latrines	158	118	276
	53.4%	39.3%	46.3%
Prepare Estimate Of The Construction And Get Technical Sanction And Administrative Approval From The District Panchayat	51	66	117
	17.2%	22.0%	19.6%
Tender The Work	10	55	65
	3.4%	18.3%	10.9%
Award And Monitor The Work	60	78	138
	20.3%	26.0%	23.2%
Promoting Health Awareness	138	188	326
	46.6%	62.7%	54.7%
Disposal Of Waste/Water Sewage	196	153	349
	66.2%	51.0%	58.6%

Source: Field Survey

Table: 5.22 Women and Child Development

	Gujarat	*Haryana*	*Total*
Disburse The Payment	8	116	124
	2.7%	38.7%	20.8%
Participation In The Implementation Of Women And Child Welfare Programmes	259	224	483
	87.5%	74.7%	81.0%
Promotion Of Health And Nutrition Programmes	241	230	471
	81.4%	76.7%	79.0%

Source: Field Survey

Welfare of weaker section and SC/ST are shown in Table 5.23. More than half of the respondents reported that they are involved in protection of weaker sections, Scheduled Caste and Scheduled Tribes from social injustice and exploitation. It was found more pronouncing in Haryana (65.3 percent) as compared to Gujarat (47.3 percent). About 2/5th respondents reported that they are coordinating and monitoring the specific programmes for the welfare of weaker sections. It was found more pronouncing in Haryana (57 percent) as compared to Gujarat (29.7 percent).

Table: 5.23 Welfare of Weaker Section and SCs/STs

	Gujarat	*Haryana*	*Total*
Coordinate And Monitor The Specific Programmes For The Welfare Of Weaker Sections	88	171	259
	29.7%	57.0%	43.5%
Protecting Such Castes And Classes From Social Injustice And Exploitation	140	196	336
	47.3%	65.3%	56.4%
Any Other	10	30	40
	3.4%	10.0%	6.7%

Source: Field Survey

Public distribution system is shown in Table 5.24. About 2/5th respondents reported that they are involved in verification of ration cards, coordination and monitoring of public distribution system and identification of beneficiaries through Village Panchayat. About 2/5th respondents were also found active in supervising and monitoring of public distribution system while more than 1/3rd respondents were found active in creation of public awareness.

Table: 5.24 Public Distribution System

	Gujarat	*Haryana*	*Total*
Supervise And Monitoring The Public Distribution System	75	151	226
	25.3%	50.3%	37.9%
Co-Ordination And Monitoring Of The Schemes	119	132	251
	40.2%	44.0%	42.1%
Identification Of Beneficiaries Through Village Panchayat	61	181	242
	20.6%	60.3%	40.6%
Verification Of Cards	88	175	263
	29.7%	58.3%	44.1%
Public Awareness	56	149	205
	18.9%	49.7%	34.4%

Source: Field Survey

Social justice and welfare of disabled is shown in Table 5.25. About half of the respondents reported that they are involved in identification of beneficiaries through Gram Sabha and coordinating and monitoring of the schemes for welfare of disabled. A significant proportion of respondents were also found active in disbursement of payments and benefits under welfare schemes and monitoring the implementation of the welfare schemes.

Table: 5.25 Social Justice and Welfare of Disabled

	Gujarat	*Haryana*	*Total*
Identify The Beneficiaries Through Gram Sabha Including Co-Ordination And Monitoring Of The Schemes	122	177	299
	41.2%	59.0%	50.2%
Disburse The Payment	35	139	174
	11.8%	46.3%	29.2%
Engage In Recover If Any	85	44	129
	28.7%	14.7%	21.6%
Monitor The Schemes	35	84	119
	11.8%	28.0%	20.0%

Source: Field Survey

The respondents were asked that whether panchayats should be given all powers to develop Panchayati Raj. Most of respondents were found in favour of complete devolution of functions, finances and functionaries to Panchayati Raj Institutions.

Table: 5.26 Whether Panchayats Should Be Given All Powers to Develop Panchayati Raj

State	*Yes*	*No*	*Total*
Gujarat	268	28	296
	90.5%	9.5%	100.0%
Haryana	278	22	300
	92.7%	7.3%	100.0%
Total	546	50	596
	91.6%	8.4%	100.0%

Source: Field Survey

Performing of roles and responsibilities of women Sarpanchs and Chairpersons of Panchayati Raj Institutions in Haryana simply demonstrates that elected women are actively participating in decentralized rural governance and decision making process. Majority of the elected women are aware about the rural development programmes, composition and types of committees and the functioning of Panchayati Raj Institutions. The elected women are also active in implementation of centrally and state sponsored scheme for rural development however, variations in perception of elected women emerges across the districts and levels of Panchayati Raj Institutions.

Chapter - 6

Problems and Challenges

Though women have been enthusiastically participating in politics but they have also been facing difficulties, challenges and problems related with their political participation and engagement and initiation of development programmes. Their low level of active participation in implementation of development programmes and schemes and also in political process is the prominent problem for the administrators and policy makers. The proxy in election process, meetings, participation in development programs and decision making has caused a serious damage to women empowerment and hence concern for all. Husbands, in-laws and close relatives have become the main decision makers relegating the actual women representatives to the background. The role conflict among these representatives has also increased while managing house responsibilities and political activities simultaneously. Since, male dominating society is reluctant in accepting the women as decision makers, they are been abused and harassed by officials, caste leaders, elected representatives and also power brokers. They are also facing revenge full attitudinal behavior in the society since they have defeated influential persons of the other sex. Thus, desire for political power, status and sustainable source of black money has also caused social concern affecting women representative. In this part of the dissertation, an attempt has been made to examine the problems and challenges faced by women Sarpanchs and Chairpersons in Panchayati Raj Institutions of Haryana.

Reasons for poor involvement of Panchayat members in planning, implementation and evaluation of development programmes are shown in Table 6.1. About 2/5the respondents reported that the main reason for poor involvement of panchayat members in planning, implementation and evaluation of development programmes is ignorance of their importance. It was found more pronouncing in Gujarat (57.1 percent) as compared to Haryana (23.7 percent). Indifferent attitude, caste factor and gender bias are other important reasons responsible for poor involvement of panchayat members in planning, implementation and evaluation of development programmes.

Table: 6.1 Reasons For Poor Involvement of Panchayat Members in Planning, Implementation and Evaluation

State	*Indifferent Attitude*	*Caste Factor*	*Gender Bias*	*Ignorance Of Their Importance*	*Good Involvement*	*Do Not Know*	*Total*
Gujarat	68	36	23	169	0	0	296
	23.0%	12.2%	7.8%	57.1%	0.0%	0.0%	100.0%
Haryana	113	21	35	71	1	59	300
	37.7%	7.0%	11.7%	23.7%	0.3%	19.7%	100.0%
Total	181	57	58	240	1	59	596
	30.4%	9.6%	9.7%	40.3%	0.2%	9.9%	100.0%

Source: Field Survey

The respondents were asked that whether women in their panchayats are involved in decision making process. Most of the respondents accepted that women are involved in decision making process in Panchayati Raj Institutions. However, 11 percent respondents reported that they are not involved in decision making process or ignored without signicicant contribution. About 60 percent respondents reported that women are providing full contribution in decision making process in Panchayati Raj Institutions. It was found more pronouncing in Gujarat (66.2 percent) as compared to Haryana (54 percent) (Table 6.2).

Table: 6.2 Whether Women Are Involved in Decision Making Process

State	*Not Involved*	*Some Way Involved*	*Ignored*	*Full Contribution*	*No Contribution*	*Total*
Gujarat	11	77	12	196	0	296
	3.7%	26.0%	4.1%	66.2%	0.0%	100.0%
Haryana	27	98	7	162	6	300
	9.0%	32.7%	2.3%	54.0%	2.0%	100.0%
Total	38	175	19	358	6	596
	6.4%	29.4%	3.2%	60.1%	1.0%	100.0%

Source: Field Survey

Attitude of male members of Panchayats towards elected women members is shown in Table 6.3. Most of the respondents reported that attitude of male members towards elected women members has been good and very good. Thus, about 7 percent respondents reported that male members are indifferent towards elected women members. This was found significantly high in Gujarat as compared to Haryana.

Table: 6.3 Attitude of Male Members of Panchayat Towards Women Panchayat Members

State	*Indifferent*	*Good*	*Very Good*	*Bad*	*Total*
Gujarat	31	119	146	0	296
	10.5%	40.2%	49.3%	0.0%	100.0%
Haryana	11	175	112	2	300
	3.7%	58.3%	37.3%	0.7%	100.0%
Total	42	294	258	2	596
	7.0%	49.3%	43.3%	0.3%	100.0%

Source: Field Survey

Measures to involve women in Panchayat affairs are shown in Table 6.4. The respondents suggested that more powers and funds should be given to women members while creation of awareness towards panchayat affairs is essential. Managerial capacity of women members should be enhanced besides believing in their capability.

Table: 6.4 Measures to Involve Women in Panchayat Activities

	Gujarat	*Haryana*	*Total*
More Powers Be Given	180	172	352
	60.8%	57.3%	59.1%
More Fund Be Given	103	107	210
	34.8%	35.7%	35.2%
More Awareness	115	204	319
	38.9%	68.0%	53.5%
Managerial Capacity Be Enhanced	84	65	149
	28.4%	21.7%	25.0%
Security Be Enhanced	42	66	108
	14.2%	22.0%	18.1%
To Believe In Their Capability	38	107	145
	12.8%	35.7%	24.3%

Source: Field Survey

Conduct of meeting of Gram Sabha and Gram Panchayat is shown in Table 6.5. Less than half of the respondents reported that they are themselves convening the meetings of Gram Panchayats and Gram Sabhas. It was found more pronouncing in Gujarat (53.4 percent) as compared to Haryana (44.3 percent). Slightly more than 2/5th respondents revealed that their husbands are convening /conducting the meetings of Gram Panchayats and Gram Sabhas. It was found more pronouncing in Haryana as compared to Gujarat. Thus, more than half of the respondents accepted that convening of Panchayat meetings is highly influenced by their close relatives.

Table: 6.5 Who Convene/Conduct Meeting of Gram Panchayat And Gram Sabha

State	*Yourself*	*Husband*	*Son*	*Father In Law*	*Any Other*	*Total*
Gujarat	158	120	6	10	2	296
	53.4%	40.5%	2.0%	3.4%	0.7%	100.0%
Haryana	133	129	29	6	3	300
	44.3%	43.0%	9.7%	2.0%	1.0%	100.0%
Total	291	249	35	16	5	596
	48.8%	41.8%	5.9%	2.7%	0.8%	100.0%

Source: Field Survey

The respondents were asked that whether they need support of any family member while attending the meetings of Gram Panchayats and Gram Sabhas. Most of the respondents revealed that they need family support while attending meetings of Village Panchayats. However, a significant proportion of respondents in Haryana reported that they do not need support of family members for attending meetings of Village Panchayats (Table 6.6).

Table: 6.6 Whether You Need Support of Family Members While Attending the Meetings of Panchayats

State	*Yes*	*No*	*Total*
Gujarat	250	46	296
	84.5%	15.5%	100.0%
Haryana	249	51	300
	83.0%	17.0%	100.0%
Total	499	97	596
	83.7%	16.3%	100.0%

Source: Field Survey

The respondents were asked that whether they are taking decisions independently in consultation with members in meetings of Village Panchayats. Most of the respondents reported that they are taking decision independently with consultation of members in the meetings of Village Panchayat. However, a significant proportion of respondents in Haryana were against the view point (Table 6.7).

The respondents were further asked that whether they consult personally to their family members for making decisions in meetings. Majority of the respondents reported that they consult their husbands personally for making decisions in panchayat meetings. This was found more pronouncing in Haryana (81.1 percent) as compared to Gujarat (60.5 percent). Other family members to whom elected women consult for making decisions in panchayats include son, mother-in-law and father-in-law (Table 6.8).

Table: 6.7 Do You Take Decision Independently With Consultation To Panches in Meetings

State	Yes	No	Total
Gujarat	280	16	296
	94.6%	5.4%	100.0%
Haryana	239	61	300
	79.7%	20.3%	100.0%
Total	519	77	596
	87.1%	12.9%	100.0%

Source: Field Survey

Table: 6.8 Whom Do You Consult Personally For Your Decisions in Meetings

State	Your Son	Your Husband	Mother In Law	Father In Law	Any Other	Total
Gujarat	27	179	56	18	16	296
	9.1%	60.5%	18.9%	6.1%	5.4%	100.0%
Haryana	40	243	0	5	12	300
	13.3%	81.0%	0.0%	1.7%	4.0%	100.0%
Total	67	422	56	23	28	596
	11.2%	70.8%	9.4%	3.9%	4.7%	100.0%

Source: Field Survey

The respondents were asked that to whom villagers approach directly for their problems. Slightly more than half of the respondents reported that villagers are approach directly to them. However, less than 2/5th respondents reported that villagers are approaching to their husbands. It was found more pronouncing in Haryana as compared to Gujarat. Thus, slightly less than half of the respondents revealed that villagers are approaching towards their family members for resolving their problems (Table 6.9).

Table: 6.9 To Whom Villagers Approach Directly For Their Problems

State	Yourself	Your Son	Your Husband	Mother In Law	Father In Law	Any Other	Total
Gujarat	159	18	104	9	4	2	296
	53.7%	6.1%	35.1%	3.0%	1.4%	0.7%	100.0%
Haryana	146	28	123	1	1	1	300
	48.7%	9.3%	41.0%	0.3%	0.3%	0.3%	100.0%
Total	305	46	227	10	5	3	596
	51.2%	7.7%	38.1%	1.7%	0.8%	0.5%	100.0%

Source: Field Survey

The respondents were further asked that whether they visit village for understanding or solution of problems. Most of the respondents revealed that they are visiting villages for understanding and solution of problems.

However, a significant proportion of respondents in Haryana revealed that they are not visiting villages for understanding or solution of village problems (Table 6.10).

Table: 6.10 Do You Visit Village For Understanding/ Solution of Problems/Issues

State	Yes	No	Total
Gujarat	290	6	296
	98.0%	2.0%	100.0%
Haryana	276	24	300
	92.0%	8.0%	100.0%
Total	566	30	596
	95.0%	5.0%	100.0%

Source: Field Survey

The respondents were asked that whether who take decision for spending money earned by them. Less than half of the respondents reported that they themselves are taking decision to spend money earned by them. It was found more pronouncing in Gujarat as compared to Haryana. About 2/5th respondents revealed that their husbands are taking decision for spending money earned by them. Thus, family members have direct bearing on decision making regarding spending of money by women elected members (Table 6.11).

Table: 6.11 Who Takes Decision for Spending Money Earned By You

State	Yourself	Your Son	Your Husband	Mother In Law	Father In Law	Any Other	Total
Gujarat	151	12	116	4	11	2	296
	51.0%	4.1%	39.2%	1.4%	3.7%	0.7%	100.0%
Haryana	138	25	122	0	6	9	300
	46.0%	8.3%	40.7%	0.0%	2.0%	3.0%	100.0%
Total	289	37	238	4	17	11	596
	48.5%	6.2%	39.9%	0.7%	2.9%	1.8%	100.0%

Source: Field Survey

The respondents were asked that whether they have separate bank account in their name. About 3/4th respondents reported that they have separate bank account on their name. It was found more pronouncing in Gujarat (92.6 percent) as compared to Haryana (58 percent). Thus, more than 2/5th respondents in Haryana revealed that they not have access to financial inclusion (Table 6.12).

Table: 6.12 Do You Have Separate Account of Your Earnings

State		*Yes*	*No*	*Total*
Gujarat		274	22	296
		92.6%	7.4%	100.0%
Haryana		174	126	300
		58.0%	42.0%	100.0%
Total		448	148	596
		75.2%	24.8%	100.0%

Source: Field Survey

The respondents were further asked that who takes decision to spend money earned by their husbands. About 46 per cent respondents reported that their husbands are taking decision to spend money earned by them. It was found more pronouncing in Haryana (59.3 percent) as compared to Gujarat (32.4 percent). However, about 29 percent respondents revealed that they are taking decision themselves to spend money earned by their husbands (Table 6.13).

Table: 6.13 Who Takes Decision To Spend The Money Earned By Your Husband

State	*Yourself*	*Your Son*	*Your Husband*	*Father In Law*	*Any Other*	*Total*
Gujarat	84	96	96	8	12	296
	28.4%	32.4%	32.4%	2.7%	4.1%	100.0%
Haryana	92	25	178	3	2	300
	30.7%	8.3%	59.3%	1.0%	0.7%	100.0%
Total	176	121	274	11	14	596
	29.5%	20.3%	46.0%	1.8%	2.3%	100.0%

Source: Field Survey

The respondents were asked that whether their opinion is taken while purchasing major household items. Most of the respondents revealed that their opinion is considered while purchasing major household items at home. Thus, elected women members are also participating actively in money centered decision making at home (Table 6.14).

The respondents were asked that who takes care of their health at home. About 46 percent respondents revealed that their husbands are taking care of their health. It was found more pronouncing in Haryana (60.7 percent) as compared to Gujarat (30.7 percent). About 20 percent respondents reported that they are taking care themselves regarding their health problems. Other family members are also taking care of health problems of elected women representatives (Table 6.15).

Table: 6.14 Whether Your Opinion is Taken While Purchasing Major Household Items in Home

State	*Yes*	*No*	*Total*
Gujarat	262	34	296
	88.5%	11.5%	100.0%
Haryana	261	39	300
	87.0%	13.0%	100.0%
Total	523	73	596
	87.8%	12.2%	100.0%

Source: Field Survey

Table: 6.15 Who Takes Care Of Your Health at Your Home

State	*Yourself*	*Your Son*	*Your Husband*	*Mother In Law*	*Father In Law*	*Any Other*	*Total*
Gujarat	70	71	91	14	38	12	296
	23.6%	24.0%	30.7%	4.7%	12.8%	4.1%	100.0%
Haryana	52	45	182	16	2	3	300
	17.3%	15.0%	60.7%	5.3%	0.7%	1.0%	100.0%
Total	122	116	273	30	40	15	596
	20.5%	19.5%	45.8%	5.0%	6.7%	2.5%	100.0%

Source: Field Survey

The respondents were asked that whether they have right to take decision about their family size. About 3/4th respondents reported that they have right to take decision regarding family planning. It was found more pronouncing in Gujarat (91.9 per cent) as compared to Haryana (60.3 percent). Thus, about 2/5th respondents in Haryana do not have right to take decision about family planning (Table 6.16).

Table: 6.16 Do You Have Right To Take Decision About Your Family Size/Planning

State	*Yes*	*No*	*Total*
Gujarat	272	24	296
	91.9%	8.1%	100.0%
Haryana	181	119	300
	60.3%	39.7%	100.0%
Total	453	143	596
	76.0%	24.0%	100.0%

Source: Field Survey

The respondents were asked that whether they are feeling free to go their parental house or to visit relatives. The overwhelming majority reported that they are free to visit their parental house or relatives. However, a significant proportion of respondents in Gujarat are not feeling free to visit their parental house or relatives (Table 6.17).

Table: 6.17 Do You Feel Free To Go Your Parental Home/Relatives

State	*Yes*	*No*	*Total*
Gujarat	242	54	296
	81.8%	18.2%	100.0%
Haryana	256	44	300
	85.3%	14.7%	100.0%
Total	498	98	596
	83.6%	16.4%	100.0%

Source: Field Survey

The respondents were further asked that whose permission is required for visiting their parental house. Most of the respondents reported that the permission of their husbands is required to visit their parental house. Permission from son, mother-in-laws and other family members is required to visit their parental house (Table 6.18).

Table: 6.18 Whose Permission is Required To Visit Your Parental House

State	*Your Son*	*Your Husband*	*Mother In Law*	*Any Other*	*Total*
Gujarat	6	44	4	0	54
	11.1%	81.5%	7.4%	0.0%	100.0%
Haryana	3	39	1	1	44
	6.8%	88.6%	2.3%	2.3%	100.0%
Total	9	83	5	1	98
	9.2%	84.7%	5.1%	1.0%	100.0%

Source: Field Survey

The respondents were asked that whether they have freedom to visit market or any other place outside of community. Most of the respondents reported that they have freedom to visit market and other places outside of the community. However, about 13 percent respondents revealed that they do not have such freedom (Table 6.19).

Table: 6.19 Do You Have Freedom To Visit Market Or Any Place Outside of Community

State	*Yes*	*No*	*Total*
Gujarat	258	38	296
	87.2%	12.8%	100.0%
Haryana	262	38	300
	87.3%	12.7%	100.0%
Total	520	76	596
	87.2%	12.8%	100.0%

Source: Field Survey

The respondents were asked that whether they are feeling any change in attitude of their family members after being elected as Sarpanch. About 55 per cent respondents reported that they are feeling change in the attitude of their family members after being elected as Sarpanch. However, about 63 percent respondents in Haryana were found against the view point (Table 6.20).

Table: 6.20 Do You Feel Any Change In Attitude of Your Family Members After Being Elected As Sarpanch

State	*Yes*	*No*	*Total*
Gujarat	216	80	296
	73.0%	27.0%	100.0%
Haryana	112	188	300
	37.3%	62.7%	100.0%
Total	328	268	596
	55.0%	45.0%	100.0%

Source: Field Survey.

Assistance in performing of household chores including looking after children is shown in Table 6.21. Majority of the respondents reported that their family members are assisting in performance of their house hold chores including caring of children. However, more than half of the respondents reported that their husbands are assisting them in performance of household chores.

Table: 6.21 Assistance in Performing of Household Chores Including Looking After Children

State	*Yourself*	*Your Son*	*Your Husband*	*Mother in Law*	*Father in Law*	*Any Other*	*Total*
Gujarat	46	26	147	46	19	12	296
	15.5%	8.8%	49.7%	15.5%	6.4%	4.1%	100.0%
Haryana	52	31	156	45	10	6	300
	17.3%	10.3%	52.0%	15.0%	3.3%	2.0%	100.0%
Total	98	57	303	91	29	18	596
	16.4%	9.6%	50.8%	15.3%	4.9%	3.0%	100.0%

Source: Field Survey

The respondents were asked that whether they face violence at home. A significant proportion of respondents in Gujarat revealed that they are also victims of domestic violence (Table 6.22).

Type of domestic violence is shown inTable 6.23. Emotional violence, physical violence, economic violence are sexual violence were reported by women elected representatives. Sexual violence was reported only in Gujarat while physical violence was reported high in Haryana as compared to Gujarat.

Table: 6.22 Do You Face Any Violence At Home By Your Husband/Family

State	*Yes*	*No*	*Total*
Gujarat	34	262	296
	11.5%	88.5%	100.0%
Haryana	3	297	300
	1.0%	99.0%	100.0%
Total	37	559	596
	6.2%	93.8%	100.0%

Source: Field Survey

Table: 6.23 Type of Domestic Violence

State	*Physical Violence*	*Emotional Violence*	*Sexual Violence*	*Economic Violence*	*Total*
Gujarat	9	17	4	4	34
	26.5%	50.0%	11.8%	11.8%	100.0%
Haryana	2	1	0	0	3
	66.7%	33.3%	0.0%	0.0%	100.0%
Total	11	18	4	4	37
	29.7%	48.6%	10.8%	10.8%	100.0%

Source: Field Survey

More than 3/4th respondents reported that Panchayati Raj Institutions have helped women. However, about 2/5th respondents in Gujarat were found against the view point (Table 6.24).

Table: 6.24 Whether Panchayati Raj Institutions Have Helped Women

State	Yes	No	Total
Gujarat	173	123	296
	58.4%	41.6%	100.0%
Haryana	294	6	300
	98.0%	2.0%	100.0%
Total	467	129	596
	78.4%	21.6%	100.0%

Source: Field Survey

The respondents were asked that whether they face discrimination towards women members by other members. About 1/4th respondents in Gujarat revealed that there is discrimination towards women members by other members in Panchayati Raj Institutions (Table 6.25).

Table: 6.25 Do You Face Discrimination Towards Women Members by Other Members

State	*Yes*	*No*	*Total*
Gujarat	70	226	296
	23.6%	76.4%	100.0%
Haryana	4	296	300
	1.3%	98.7%	100.0%
Total	74	522	596
	12.4%	87.6%	100.0%

Source: Field Survey

The respondents were asked that whether reservation of seats for women is required. Most of the respondents were found in favour of reservation for women in political institutions (Table 6.26).

Table: 6.26 Whether Reservation of Seats For Women is Required

State	*Yes*	*No*	*Total*
Gujarat	284	12	296
	95.9%	4.1%	100.0%
Haryana	299	1	300
	99.7%	0.3%	100.0%
Total	583	13	596
	97.8%	2.2%	100.0%

Source: Field Survey

Most of the respondents were of the view that more powers should be given to women and sensitization and awareness creation among women regarding Panchayat activities should be ensured for their active involvement. Capacity building of elected women panchayat members has also been suggested by a significant proportion of respondents. About $2/5^{th}$ respondents were in favour of devolving more funds to panchayats. Elected women Sarpanchs and Chairpersons also face problems and challenges in performing their assigned duties and responsibilities. They face role conflicts as they have to perform the dual role both at domestic and panchayat fronts. The influence of family members in convening, conducting and decision making in panchayats is still high while villagers are directly approaching to the family members of elected women panchayat members for solving their problems. The household responsibilities and duties are no doubt shared by other family members however, elected women members do not enjoy full freedom for visiting their relatives and parental house as well as participation in child centred and money centred decisions in family.

Chapter - 7

Conclusion and Suggestions

Women empowerment is the buzzword now-a-days. No country can afford development without considering women who constitute about half of its stock of human resource. However, development has bypassed women in India despite worshiping and paying respect to women in mythology and historical texts. Gender disparities vary vastly across cultural, geographical and historical context. India is a large country with vast economic and socio-cultural diversity in its varied regions. The development issues related to women in a large country like India will not only be inappropriate but sometimes even misleading. Women specific and women related legislations have been enacted to safeguard the rights and interest of women, besides protecting against discrimination, violence, and atrocities and also to prevent socially undesirable practices. Empowerment of women is closely linked to the opportunities they have in education, health, employment and for political participation. Over the years, significant advancements have been made in India on many of these counts. Data on literacy rates, enrolment and drop rates in primary education, life expectancy, infant mortality, maternal mortality rates, etc has shown a progressive trend. However, other parameters that reflect the status and position of women in society such as work participation rates, sex ratio in the age group of 0-6 years and gender based violence continue to be heavily skewed against women .New challenges such as increased intra-country migration, changing labour markets requiring new skill sets and rapidly changing technology have also emerged.

Empowerment of women is a socio-political ideal, encompassing notions of dignity and equality, envisioned in relation to the wider framework of women's rights. It is a process of gaining control over self, over resources and over existing societal perceptions and attitudes and would be achieved only when an improvement in the 'condition' of women is accompanied by an advancement in their 'position' by enlarging the economic, social and political freedoms and choices available to them. The National Policy for the Empowerment of Women, 2001 viewed empowerment as an enabling process that must lead to their economic as well as social transformation. Government has sought to operationalise this approach through legislative and programmatic interventions as well as by mainstreaming gender into the development planning process. Numerous such initiatives were taken during the Eleventh Plan period. These initiatives need to be consolidated and built on during the Twelfth Five Year Plan to enable women to challenge and change the contexts in which they live. Focussed efforts through development programmes, both multi sectoral as well as targeted, along with governance reforms would be a pre-requisite. Women, especially the vulnerable and marginalized, would need to be provided a level playing field to access social, economic and legal entitlements as a right.

India is the world's largest democracy triggered by the 73rd and 74th amendments to the Constitution. The reservation of one-third seats for women has resulted in more than a million women elected women leaders in decision making positions at grassroots levels. With the reservation already increased to 50 percent in several states, e.g., Bihar, Chhattisgarh, Madhya Pradesh, Kerala, Rajasthan and a Constitutional amendment to this effect in the process, the Panchayats will have great potential for women's empowerment and their contribution to gender sensitive good governance. While affirmative action in terms of reservation for ensuring women's political representation is an imperative step, it is not adequate to promote women's leadership and their participation in governance. However, women face social, economic and various other forms of institutional barriers to entering local governments and even in performing their duties as elected representatives. Efforts are being made to establish linkages between women functionaries at the local level such as EWRs, AWW, ASHA, teachers and women members of SHGs so that they can be empowered by working collectively with a shared sense of solidarity. Involvement of NYK and NSS volunteers in supporting EWRs for social change will be encouraged.

The imperatives of decentralized planning in India have been repeatedly emphasized in the Five Year Plan documents in our country. However, the progress in this direction remained slow and faltering despite frequent changes in the policy prescriptions. The most important reason attributable to the half-hearted or incomplete implementation of the process of decentralized planning was that the required procedures and organizations were not set-up in the right perspective and real efforts worth the name were also not made to operationalize the process of decentralized planning.

Needless to mention here, that only a few states of the country have really taken concrete steps to decentralize the process of planning at the district level, particularly after the Fifth Five Year Plan. These efforts have been examined in detail by the working group on district planning set-up by the Planning Commission which also forwarded comprehensive suggestion for the operationalization of decentralized planning.

As we approach 21st Century Indian polity has been striving for establishing democratic goals through modernizing its political and administrative institutions. With a change in development paradigms, the focus of development planning has shifted to participatory development with social justice and equity. It called for decentralized administration, ensuring people's participation in decision making and giving priorities to their local needs. The 73rd and 74th Constitutional Amendment Acts 1992 made the provision for ensuring local self governance through empowering local bodies. Thus, the units of the Local Self-Government were given statutory status and state governments were given the mandatory provisions for establishing Panchayats at three tiers. Importantly, the local bodies have become the units of the government to have a share in decision making and active participation in development process for socio-economic development of the region. Though, the provision of local bodies particularly, Panchayats may be traced out in the historical text, monuments and excavation sites. The role of Panchayats in development has been found praiseworthy in ancient period, however, the credit for strengthening of Panchayats in modern period goes to Britishers. Due to lack of financial and functional autonomy, the Panchayats could not perform well, and because of non-statutory status of Panchayats, State Governments had no mandatory powers to establish the units of Local Self Government. With the enactment of State Conformity Amendment Act 1994, the process of functional and financial devolution to the local bodies was initiated by the State Governments.

State local fiscal relations in the context of 73rd and 74th Amendment Acts have acquired a new meaning and significance. The inadequacy of finances has been a major impediment in the effective functioning of local bodies in India. Their financial position is being revamped through the mechanism of State Finance Commissions. The existing sources of Panchayats at all levels are highly inadequate to meet out their fiscal needs. Therefore, the task of State Finance Commissions has become more difficult and challenging one. Though, functions and finances have been devolved to local bodies but there is mismatch between them. Even though, funds have been transferred by Union Finance Commissions and State Finance

Commissions to local bodies, these bodies face fiscal deficit and there are serious challenges to sustain and maintain core services and to fulfill the committed liabilities by the Panchayats. Therefore, there is an urgent need to assess the potential of Panchayat finances and suggesting policy measures for augmenting their resources.

Decentralized governance in Post 1992 scenario has made available the opportunities for empowering women, weaker sections, poor and implementation of participatory rural development paradigms. Moreover, new Panchayat Raj System has introduced the concept of local development planning, participatory development and people's centred governance and development. The decentralized governance has focused on empowerment of Panchayat functionaries, representatives and concerned officials of rural development departments. However, they need orientation, training and special education to cope up with new changes, challenges and opportunities unleashed by new economic and administrative environment. The capacity building of development functionaries is needed for effective functioning of local bodies, administration of development of programmes, and enhancing efficiency, effectiveness and productivity both of individuals and institutions. Moreover, the process of political and fiscal decentralization has to be completed within the target time framework with strong political and administrative will. Again, the rural Panchayats are needed to be strengthened to ensure the concept of good governance, effective and active participation in governance of rural development programmes and schemes as well as functioning of grassroots level democratic units of government.

Major Findings

- Most of the respondents were from the middle age group and from General castes. However, proportion of women respondents from General communities and Scheduled Castes was also reported to be significant. Most of the respondents were from Hindu communities.
- Most of the respondents were married however, their educational levels were reported to be poor as about 11 per cent respondents were graduates and above. Majority of the respondents reported that they received their education from co-educational institutions.
- Majority of the respondents were from joint families. The family main occupation was reported agriculture and labour. The main profession of respondents was reported to be housewives. Agriculture, private service labour and petty business were the main profession of the spouses of respondents.

- About 1/3rd respondents revealed that they do not own agriculture land while majority of the respondents reported that the size of their landholdings is small. Majority of the respondents further revealed that their monthly family income is less than ₹ 30,000.
- Most of the respondents reported that they were elected for the first time. Majority of the respondents further reported that they were elected as reserved candidates in the Panchayat Elections however; about 32 percent respondents were from General categories. About 63 percent respondents reported that they were elected against the seats reserved for women. About half of the respondents reported that they do not have experience in active politics while majority of the respondents having political experience said that they have experience of only a few years.
- Less than 2/5th respondents reported that they are affiliated with political parties. However, the influence of their spouses in Panchayat election was recorded significantly high.
- The main reasons for poor involvement of Panchayat members in implementation of development programmes were reported to be indifferent attitude, ignorance of their importance and lack of awareness about the development programmes as well as gender bias. More than half of the respondents reported that women are involved in decision making process as they are contributing significantly. However, about 10 percent respondents reported that women are not involved in decision making process.
- The attitude of male members of Panchayat towards women Panchayat members has been reported to be good and very good. However, a small proportion of respondents revealed that male members of Panchayat are indifferent towards them. Thus, most of the respondents were in favour of devolving more powers to Panchayat and enhancing the budgetary allocations to local governments besides creation of awareness regarding development programmes and schemes.
- About half of the respondents reported that they are themselves convening the meetings of Panchayats however; they need support of family members while attending the meetings of Panchayat. Most of the respondents reported that they are taking decisions independently with consultation to the members of Panchayats.
- Most of the respondents reported that villagers are approaching directly to them and their relatives for their problems. Most of the

respondents revealed that they are also visiting the villages for understanding of problems and developmental issues.

- About 48 percent respondents reported that they are themselves taking decision for spending of money earned by them however, their spouses and sons are also taking decisions for spending money earned by their wives or mothers. About 75 per cent respondents reported that they own separate bank account for their earnings. About 29 percent respondents reported that they are taking decisions for spending money earned by their spouses.
- Most of the respondents reported that their opinion is being sought while purchasing the major household items. The family members are also taking care the health of women at home. The respondents also revealed that they have rights to take decision about family planning and they feel free to visit their parental house, relatives and markets.
- Elected women are actively participating in decentralized rural governance and decision making process. A large proportion of the elected women are aware about the rural development programmes, composition and types of committees and the functioning of Panchayati Raj Institutions.
- The elected women are also active in implementation of centrally and state sponsored schemes for rural development however, a variation in perception of elected women emerges across the districts and levels of Panchayati Raj Institutions.
- About 55 percent respondents reported that they are feeling changes in the attitude of their family members after elected as Sarpanch/ Chairperson. They are also receiving assistance in performing of household chores and caring of children.
- Most of the respondents reported that reservation of women in Panchayati Raj Institutions has really helped in empowerment of women. Most of the respondents were of the view that reservation of seats for women in Panchayati Raj Institutions is necessary for their empowerment and upliftment.

Suggestions

- Women empowerment must be holistic universal and participative in order to insure inclusive and in situ growth and development of the Nation. Road map of minority women empowerment, dealing with different sectors of economy should be prepared keeping in view of the futuristic vision.

- In older to ensure the effective enforcement of legislations and constitution provisions, budgetary support should be given to create and strengthen the required infrastructure.
- Special emphasis should be given to promote the employment opportunities for minority women in those sectors of economy which have been leading the economic growth in the country such as information technology, telecommunication, bio-technology, etc.
- India needs to continually investment in skills and knowledge development and training for their workforce in light of global changes, including advances in technology and work organizations. Human resources development or human capital formation are essential for sustaining a productive workforce.
- A societal reorientation for gender just society would require a radical transformation through awareness on gender issues and sustained efforts of imparting training and education on various developmental activities. Women's own perceptions about themselves also need to be changed; besides a positive role played by media and related organizations.
- Though the National Policy on Women has detailed out women's rights to productive resources, their access to land, credit, finance, insurance, etc., all these remain severely constrained. Moreover, state women policy should be drafted and implemented in each state ensuring a higher allocation on the women development programmes. In order to ensure proper and effective functioning of women oriented programmes and schemes, judicious allocation of budgetary resources is imperative a gender budgeting as a tool for women empowerment is gaining importance.
- The participation of local people in identification of Panchayats as reserved for women candidates should be ensured by the government officials at village, block and district Panchayats and adequate time should be provided for nomination of candidature for contesting election.
- There should be criteria of minimum qualification for candidates willing to contest the Panchayat election both for Sarpanch and Chairperson of Panchayat Samiti and Zila Parishad. Educated women representatives in local governments are expected to play crucial role in decision making process and implementation of rural development programmes.

- There should be more emphasis on holding the meetings of Panchayats with ensuring an encouraging the participation of every women Sarpanch/Chairperson of Village Panchayat, Panchayat Samiti and Zila Parishad. The elected representatives should be motivated to take active part in the discussions and deliberations on policy decisions in various committees.
- Women representatives need training and capacity building for enhancing their leadership quality, independency culture and self confidence besides awareness about the Constitutional rights and functions and duties as provided to PRI's representatives under Panchayati Raj System, nature of Indian democracy and Constitutional policies and programmes for women, rural development and social welfare programmes and schemes, etc.
- There is need of increasing emphasis on more women related welfare schemes and development programmes for strengthening the involvement of women in implementation of development programmes and schemes in rural areas.
- Promotion and encouragement of the formation and strengthening of social institutions such as Women's Associations, SHGs, Mahila Mangal Dal, Mahila Manch, Women Headed Civil Socities, etc. will create opportunities for women empowerment and ensure the participation of women in different developmental activities.
- The attitude of male members towards women's entry into politics has to be changed through orientation courses and training programmes for officials and elected representatives, both males and females. Besides, there is a need to train the women leaders at regular intervals to enable them to manage the responsibilities assigned to them in the Panchyats at all the levels.
- There is need to increase efforts required for real empowerment of rural women to bring about an attitudinal change in both men and women. The feeling that women are meant for household activities and rearing children needs to be replaced by a feeling of equal partnership of women and men.
- The women should also be encouraged to organize themselves. The Mahila Mandals in the villages can be effectively used as instruments to mobilize them for this purpose. Some successful women's organizations can also act as catalytic agents for encouraging women's participation in social and political activities. The government should provide finance and infrastructure to

some of the successful women organizations to take up the responsibility of encouraging the women elected representatives. This task could also be taken up by the leaders of women's movement in the country. They too can provide support to sensitize the rural women.

- Incentives play a vital role in ensuring the participation of elected representatives in decision-making. It has been noticed that there are certain very active and enlightened women leaders at all the levels of Panchayats, who have been successfully implementing the developmental schemes and have ensured overall development of their constituencies. Such leaders need to be encouraged by publicizing their leadership qualities and honouring them in public meetings. It will certainly encourage other women representatives and their cusses stores and good practices will get replicated.
- The genuine NGOs should be identified for entrusting them the tasks of training, encouraging, organizing, mobilizing and guiding the elected women representatives. National Literacy Mission and other organizations engaged in the Sarva Shiksha Abhiyan should also be assigned the responsibility of educating the rural masses in general and the rural women in particular regarding the significance of Panchyati Raj and empowerment of women.
- The media both print as well as electronic can play an important role in creating awareness in the rural society. It can act as an agent of political socialization for inculcating the values of gender quality and gender justice.
- The unfinished agenda of women empowerment should be finished by enacting an Amendment for providing reservation for women in the national parliament and the state legislatures. The reservations at local level are not enough for women empowerment.
- India should adopt a broad policy framework including growth with equity, improving governance through participation of poor and collaboration with all stakeholders in planning process and regional cooperation to remove trade barriers and eliminating harmful taxes and competition practices.
- A strong focus is needed on economic and social rights and on their implementation. Support mechanisms are needed for women to claim legal entitlements.
- India needs to continually investment in skills and knowledge development and training for their workforce in light of global changes, including advances in technology and work organizations.

Human resources development or human capital formation are essential for sustaining a productive workforce.

- Strengthening national mechanisms and promoting the greater participation of women in community based and non-government organizations remain one of the major objectives in empowering women. Social development in general and social integration in particular, forms the broad frameworks within which the women's organizations are working in advancing the cause of women.
- Promoting the greater participation of women in decision making process remains another major objective towards the goal of empowering women. Thus, it is imperative to create more opportunities for women to participate in the institutions of government.
- A societal reorientation for gender just society would require a radical transformation through awareness on gender issues and sustained efforts of imparting training and education on various developmental activities. Women's own perceptions about themselves also need to be changed; besides a positive role played by media and related organizations.
- Women's access to paid work may give them a greater sense of self reliance and greater purchasing power. Similarly, women's presence in the governance structures of society clearly carries the potential to change unjust practices. Thus, it is imperative to create more opportunities for women to participate in decision making process and governance of development programmes.
- The gender disaggregated database has to be created and strengthened in the local governments including parastatal agencies, which will enable better analysis and more effective monitoring of targets and achievements for men and women.
- A system should be set up to collate gender disaggregated data from relevant departments to obtain the gender-wise relevant statistical data base, targets and fiscal and financial achievements. A gender audit of plans, policies and programmes of various local governments with pro-women allocations must be conducted for the impact assessment of the programmes and schemes.
- Elected People's Representatives in local governments must necessarily be brought under the purview of gender sensitization processes besides including district level officials such as District Collectors, DDOs, Commissioners, and BDOs, District Social Welfare Officers, line department officials, District Local Fund Auditor (DLFAs) and ULB / Panchayat functionaries.

Bibliography

Abhayaratna, Manel. (2008), "Empowerment of Women: Who Cares" Daily Mirror, March 11.

Agarwal, Rashmi & Rao, B.V.L.N. (2004), Gender Issues: A Road Map to Empowerment, Shipra Publications, New Delhi.

Agrawal, Amba (2005), Fiscal Decentralization in India: An Inter-State Analysis of Panchayat Finances, Serials Publications, New Delhi.

Ahikire, (2003) 'Gender Equity and Local Democracy in Uganda: Addressing the Challenge of Women's Political Effectiveness in Local Government', in Anne Marie Goetz and Shireen Hassim (eds), No Shortcuts to Power: African Women in Politics and Policy-Making, Zed Books, London.

Ahmed, Imtiaz (1975), "Women in Politics", in Devaki Jain (Ed.), Indian Women, Publications division, New Delhi.

Akerkar, S (1995), "Theory and Practice of Women's Movement in India: A Discourse Analysis", Economic & Political Weekly, Vol XXX, No 27.

Almond, G.A. G.B. Powell Jr. (1975) Comparative Politics: A Developmental Approach, Amerind Publishing Company, New Delhi, p. 98.

Almond, G.A. and Verba, S. (1965) The Civic Culture: Political Attitude and Democracy in Five Nations. Boston: Little Brown P 119.

Andrews, A. Julio. (1999), "Nepal" Strengthening Democracy Through Women's Political Participation, The Asian Foundation Publication.

Arora, Banarsi (1999), "Women in Politics: Governance in Patriarchal and Non-participatory Culture", Guru Nanak Journal of Sociology, 20 (1-2).

Bachhi, C. (2001), Managing Equity: Mainstreaming and Diversity in Australian Universities, IN A Brooks & Mclnnon (Ed.).

Bala, Raj (1997) The Legal and Political Status of Women in India, Mohit Publications, New Delhi, , p. 250.

Balmori Hofbaur Helena (2003), Gender and Budgets, Overview Report, Bridge, University of Sussex, February.

Banerjee, Mukta, (1998) Women in Local Governance: Macro Myths, Micro Realities' Social Change, Vol. 28, No. 1.

Banerjee, Mukta, (1998), Women in Local Governance: Macro Myths, Micro Realities' Social Change, Vol. 28, No. 1.

Banerjee, Sikata (2003), "Gender and Nationalism: The Masculinisation of Hinduism and Female Political Participation in India", Women's Studies International Forum, 26 (2).

Banthia, J.K. (2003), "Parsi demography: past, recent and future", Parzor Seminar, 4th October, 2003, Mumbai.

Bari, Farzana. (2005), "Women's Political Participation: Issues and Challenges" (United Nations: DAW, Expert Meeting Group, Bangkok, Thailand, 8-11 Nov.

Baseline Report (1998), "Women and Political Participation in India" prepared by NIAS et al and coordinated by IWRAW Asia Pacifi c, advanced unedited version.

Basu, Amrita (1992), Two Faces of Protest: Contrasting Modes of Women's Activism in India (Berkeley: University of California Press).

Basu, Durga Das (1998), Introduction to the Constitution of India, Prentice – Hall of India, New Delhi.

Batliwalla, Srilatha (1996), "Transforming of Political Culture" Economic and Political Weekly, XXXI, Number 21.

Belington, Julie. (2004), "The Implementation of Quotas: African Experiences" Quota Report Series (IDEA Publications).

Bhatkal, Svati, (1997) 'Andhra Pradesh: The Great Betrayal', The Voice of People Awakening, April 1.

Brar, Manpreet Kaur (2013), Political Participation And Representation Of Women In State Assemblies, International Journal Of Behavioral Social And Movement Sciences, Vol. 2, No. 04.

Brush, C.G., Carter, N.M., Gatewood, E.J., Greene, P.G., & Hart, M.M. (Eds). (2006). "growth oriented women entrepreneurs and their businesses: a global research perspective", Cheltenham, UK: edward elgar publishing ltd.

Buch, Nirmala, (2000) 'Women's Experience in New Panchayats: The Emerging Leadership of Rural Women', Centre for Women's Development Studies, Occasional Paper No. 35, New Delhi.

Burns, Nancy, Kay Lehman Schlozman, and Sidney Verba, (2001) The Private Roots of Public Action: Gender, Equality, and Political Participation, Harvard University Press, Cambridge, Massachusetts.

CARE India (2007), Microfinance and Women's Empowerment: Programme and Policy Review, Policy and Advocacy, Rashtriya Mahila Kosh, New Delhi

Centre for Voting and Democracy, (2003) 'Women in Legislatures Around the World, 2003', http://www. fairvote. org/ women/ women comparison 03. htm.

CENWOR, (1994) Women's Political Empowerment and Decision Making, Centre for Women's Research, Colombo.

Chanana Karuna (2007), "Globalization, Higher Education and Gender: Changing Subject Choices of Indian Women Students", Economic and Political Weekly, Vol.42, No.7.

Chattopadhyay, Raghabendra, and Esther Duflo, (2001) 'Women as Policy-Makers: Evidence from a India-Wide Randomized Policy Experiment', mimeo Department of Economics, Massachusetts Institute of Technology.

Chhibber, Pradeep (2002), "Why Are Women Politically Active? The Household, Public Space, and Political Participation in India", www. world vauesurvey. org.

Chowdhury, Dr Najma. (2002), "The Implementation of Quotas: Bangladesh Experience- Dependence and Marginality in Politics", Quota Report Series, IDEA Publications.

Clarke, J.R. (1996), Educational Equity in Higher Education: An International Perspective, IN G.D. Postle et.al., Towards Excellence and Diversity: Educational Equity in the Australian Higher Sector in 1995, USQ Press, Queensland.

Cleland, J. and J.Hobcraft, (1985). Reproductive Change in Developing Countries: Insight from the World Fertility, London, Oxford Press.

Closky. Herbert M.C. (1968) "Political Participation" International Encyclopedia of Social Sciences vol:12 (New York: MacMillan , p. 253.

Crook, R.C. and J. Manor (1998), Democracy and Decentralization in South Asia and West Africa, Cambridge University Press, Cambridge.

Crook, R.C. and Sverrisson, A.S. (2001), "Decentralization and Poverty Alleviation in Developing Countries: A Comparative Analysis", IDS Working Paper 130, Institute of Development Studies, Brighton.

Dahlerup, Drude. (2006), Women Quotas and Politics, London: Routledge

Darcy, R., Susan Welch, and Janet Clark, (1994) Women, Elections, and Representation, University of Nebraska Press, Lincoln.

Darcy, R., Susan Welch, and Janet Clark, (1994), Women, Elections, and Representation, University of Nebraska Press, Lincoln.

Das, . Hari Hara (1987) 1ntroduc:ion to Political Sociology, Vikas Publishing House, New Delhi, , p. 146.

Davis et. al (1994) Decentralization by Default : Local Government and The View From Villages in Gambia , Public Administration and Development , Vol.14 , No 3.

Desai S and V Kulkarni (2010), "Unequal Playing Field: Socio-religious Inequalities in Educational Attainment" in Basant R and Shariff, A (eds.) (2010), Handbook of Muslims in India: Empirical and Policy Perspectives, Oxford University Press.

Deshpande, Rajeshwari (2004), "How Gendered Was Women's Participation Women in Election 2004", Economic & Political Weekly, Vol. 39 (51).

Development Alternatives (2015) Achieving The Sustainable Development Goals in India : A Study of Financial requirements and Gaps, development Alternatives, New Delhi

Dhawan, G. & Singh, B.(1991), "Gender Issues: A Study of Decision Making Process in Rainfed Agriculture", Paper presented at International Conference on Extension Strategy for Minimizing Risk in Rainfed Agriculture, New Delh.

Dhawan, G. (1995), "Human Security and Sustainable Development", Kurukshetra, August.

Dighe, Anita, (1993) 'Women, Literacy and Empowerment: The Nellore Experience', Paper Presented at the International Seminar on 'Women, Education, and Empowerment' held at UNESCO Institute for Education, Hamburg, 27 January – 2 February.

Dowse, R. and Hughes, J. (1971) "Girls, Boys and Politics", British Journal of Sociology, Vol.22, P 53-65.

Dowse, Robert E. (1972) Political Sociology, John Wiley and Sons, London, p.290.

Dubey, M.P. & Padalia, Munni (Ed) (2002), Democratic Decentralization And Panchayati Raj In India, Anamika Pub., Delhi.

Elson Diana (2002) , Gender Responsive Budget Initiatives: Key Dimensions and Practical Examples, Heinrich-Boell Foundation, Berlin, February.

Elson, Diane (1999) Integrating Gender Issues into National Budget Polices & Procedures: Some Policy Options, Journal of International Development, Vol. 10.

Equity Foundation (2006), Women: Struggle for Existence, Equity Foundation, Patna.

Forbes, Geraldine (1979), "Votes for Women: The Demand for Women's Franchise, 1917-1937" in Vine Majumdar (ed.), Symbols of Power: Studies in the Political Status of Women in India (Bombay: Allied Publishers Private Ltd).

Gender Resource Centre (2018) Status Report on Gender Budgeting in Bihar, Gender Resource Centre, Women Development Corporation, Deptt. of Social Welfare, Government of Bihar, Patna.

Ghimir, Dogra. (2006), "South Asian Situation on Women in Politics" Paper Presented at the 6th Asia Pacific Congress on Political Empowerment of Women Organize by the Center for Asia – Pacific Women in Politics in Manila 10-12 Feb. Women's Studies Journal, Volume 23 Number 1, September 2009: 19-35. ISSN 1173-6615 © 2009 Women's Studies Association of New Zealand Hosted at www.wsanz.org. nz/.

Gleason, Suzanne (2001), "Female Political Participation and Health in India", Annals AAPPS, 573.

Government of Bihar (2019) Women and Girls in Bihar – Taking Stock , looking Ahead : A Gender Report Card, Centre for Catalyzing Change and Women development Corporation, Deptt. of social welfare, Government of Bihar, Patna.

Government of India (2006), Planning Commission, Report of the Steering Committee on Empowerment of Women and Development of Children for the Eleventh Plan.

Government of India (2007) Gender Budgeting Handbook for Government of India, Ministries & Departments, Ministry of Women and Child Development, Govt. of India.

Government of India (2009), Gendering Human Development Indices: Recasting the Gender Development Index and Gender Empowerment Measure for India, Ministry of Women and Child Development, Government of India.

Government of India (2010), Engendering Public Policy for the 11th Five Year Plan, Planning Commission, Government of India, New Delhi.

Government of India (2010), Planning Commission, Engendering Public Policy: A Report on the Work of the Working Group of Feminist Economists during the Preparation of the Eleventh Five Year Plan, 2007-2012, May.

Government of India (2012), Report of Steering Committee on Empowerment of Women and Development of Children for 12th Plan, Ministry of Women and Child Development, Government of India, New Delhi.

Government of India (2012), Working Group Report on Women Agency for 12th Plan, Ministry of Women and Child Development, Government of India, New Delhi.

Government of India (2013) National Urban Livelihood Mission, Draft Mission Document, Ministry of Housing and Urban Poverty Alleviation, Government of India, New Delhi.

Government of India (2013), "Twelfth Five-Year Plan", Planning Commission, New Delhi.

Government of India (2012) Engendering Public Policy, Ministry of Women and Child Development, Government of India.

Harper, Malcolm (1998), Gender, Economic Growth, And Poverty, In Women And Economic Policy By Barbara Evers, Oxfam Focus On Gender, Oxfam.

Helan, D. (2001) General Manual: A Practical Guide for Development Policy Makers and Practitioners, DFID, London.

Helena, Hofbauer Balmori (2003) Gender and Budgets: Overview Report , Institute of Development Studies, Sussex.

Hughes, K D. et. al (2012) Extending Women's Entrepreneurship Research in New Directions , Entrepreneurship Theory and Practice , Vol. 36 No. 2.

Huntington, S.P. (1992), The Third Wave: Decentralization in the Late Twentieth Century, University of Oklahoma Press, London.

IDASA, (1997) 'Elections Fact Sheet', Institute for Democratic Alternatives in South Africa, Cape Town.

IDEA (2003), International Institute for Democracy and Electoral Assistance, "The implementation of quotas: Asian Experience" quota workshops report series Jakarta Indonesia 25 Sep 2002, IDEA Publications.

Inter-Parliamentary Union, (1997) Democracy Still in the Making: Men and Women in Politics, IPU, Geneva.

Jane, P. (2002) Gender and Empowerment: New Thoughts and New Approaches, In Vandana Desai and Robert B. Porrter (Ed). The Companion to Development Studies, Arnold, London.

Jayawardena, Kishali Pinto, (2003) 'Proportional Representation, Political Violence and the Participation of Women in the Political Process in Sri Lanka', in Sunil Bastian and Robin Luckham (eds), Can Democracy Be Designed? The Politics of Institutional Choice in Conflict-torn Societies, London: Zed Publishing.

Jayaweera, Swarna, (1997) 'Women, Education, and Empowerment in Asia', Gender and Education, Vol. 9, No. 4.

Jenkin, Rober, (1997) Democratic Adjustment: Explaining the Political Sustainability of Economic Reform in India, University of Sussex.

Jenkins, Laura Dudley (2003), Identity and Identification in India – Defining the Disadvantaged ,London: Routledge Curzon.

Jonasdottir, G. Anna. (1998), is There a Nordic Feminism, Nordic Feminist Thought on Culture and Society, London: Routledge.

Karl Marlee (1995), Women and Empowerment: Participation and Decision Making, Zed Books Ltd., London and New Jersey.

Keiser, Lael R., Vicky M. Wilkins, Kenneth J. Meier, and Catherine A. Holland, (2002), 'Lipstick and Logarithms: Gender, Institutional Context, and Representative Bureaucracy', American Political Science Review, Vol. 96, No. 3.

Kenworthy, Lane, and Melissa Malami, (1999) 'Gender Inequality in Political Representation: A Worldwide Comparative Analysis', Social Forces, Vol. 78, No. 1.

Khosla, Renu (2000) Women and Sanitation: The Urban Reality. Experiences of Government Programmes, NGOs and CBOs. Social Change. CSD. Vol. 30, pp. 1&2, New Delhi.

Khosla, Renu (2009) Addressing Gender Concerns in India's Urban Renewal Mission, United Nations Development Programme (UNDP).

Kishore, Sunita & Gupta, K. (2004), Women's Empowerment in India and its States, Economic & Political Weekly, Feb. 14.

Kishwar, Madhu (1996), "Women and Politics: Beyond Quotas", Economic & Political Weekly, XXXI, Number 43.

Kudva, Neema, (2003) 'Engineering Elections: The Experiences of Women in *Panchayati* Raj in Karnataka, India', International Journal of Politics, Culture, and Society, Vol. 16, No. 3.

Kuensel, (2007), Editorial, "Make Way for Women", December, 12.

Kulke, E. (1974). The Parsees in India: A Minority as Agent of Social Change, Delhi, Vikas Publishing House, Pvt. Ltd.

Kumar, R., (1994) "Development and Women's Work in Kerala", Interaction and Paradoxes", Economic and Political Weekly (Mumbai), Dec.17-24.

Lane, R.E. (1961) Political Life. Illinois: The Free Press. P 209.

Lingam, Lakshmi and Krishnaraj, Maithreyi (2010) , Maternity Protection in India: A National Assessment. Study Commissioned by the Ministry of Labour and Employment, Government of India, New Delhi and ILO. New Delhi.

Lipjart, Arend, (1991) 'Debate – Proportional Representation III. Double-Checking the Evidence', Journal of Democracy, Vol. 42.

Lock, M (1998), "Situating Women in the Politics of Health" in S Sherwin et al (ed.), The Politics of Women's Health: Exploring Agency and Autonomy (Philadelphia: Temple University Press).

Lopez August and Saadia Zahidi (2005), Women Empowerment: Measuring the Global Gender Gap, World Economic Forum, Switzerland.

Lorimer, F. (1954), Culture and Human Fertility, United Nations Educational, Scientific and Cultural Organization, Paris.

Lovenduski, Joni, and Pippa Norris, (Eds) (1993) Gender and Party Politics, Sage, London.

Macgill , N. Frank (2002) International Encyclopaedia of Government and Politics, Volume Two, New Delhi: S. Chand & Company Ltd, , p. 1016.

Manor, J., (1979), The Failure of Political Integration in Sri Lanka, Journal of Commonwealth and Comparative Politics, 17(1).

Manor, James (1981), Party Decay and Political Crisis in India, The Washington Quarterly, Summer.

Marshall, Ann, (2002) 'Organizing Across the Divide: Local Feminist Activism, Everyday Life, and the Election of Women to Public Office', Social Science Quarterly, Vol. 83, No. 3.

Matland, E. Richard (2004), "The Norwegian Experience of Gender Quotas", A paper presented at the International Institute for Democracy and electoral Assistance (IDEA) CEE Network for Gender issues conference. Budapest, Hungary, 22-23 October 2004.

Matland, Richard E. and Michelle Taylor, (1997) 'Electoral System Effects on Women's Representation', Comparative Political Studies, Vol. 30.

Matland, Richard E., (1998) 'Women's Representation in National Legislatures: Developed and Developing Countries', Legislative Studies Quarterly, Vol. 23.

Mayaram, Shail, (1999) 'Backlash Against Women in the Panchayat System', unpublished mimeo, Institute for Development Studies, Jaipur.

Mayaram, Shail, and Pritam Pal, (1996) 'The Politics of Women's Reservation: Women Panchayat Representatives in Rajasthan, Performance, Problems, and Potential', Institute of Development Studies Jaipur Working Paper No. 074, Jaipur.

Mbatha, Likhapha (2003) 'Democratizing Local Government: Problems and opportunities in the Advancement of Gender Equality in South Africa', in Anne Marie Goetz and Shireen Hassim (eds), No Shortcuts to Power: African Women in Politics and Policy-Making, Zed Books, London.

McClosky, H. (1968) Political Participation. In International Encyclopaedia of the Social Sciences, New York Collier- Macmillan, Vol. 12, P 253.

McDonagh, Eileen, (2002) 'Political Citizenship and Democratization: The gender Paradox', American Political Science Review, Vol. 96, No. 3.

Mckenna, Mark Reade, "Sri Lanka" Strengthening Democracy Through women's political Participation, The Asian Foundation Publication.

Milbrath, L. (1965) Political Participation, Chicago: Rand Me Nally. P 32.

Milbrath, Lester W. M.L. Goel, (1977) Political Participation: How and Why Do People Get Involved in Politics, Rand Mcnally, Chicago,, p. 2.

Mishra Yamini (2010), Gender – Responsive Budgeting as a Tool for Alternative Economic Planning, IN In Search of Economic Alternatives for Gender and Social Justice: Voices from India Edited by Wichterich, C., Heinrich Boll Stiftung – Wide, Brussels, Belgium.

Mishra, Yamini & Bhumika Jhamb (2007) What Does Budget 2007-08 Offer Women?, Economy & Political Weekly, April, 21.

Mishra, Yamini and Navanita Sinha (2012) "Gender Responsive Budgeting in India: What Has Gone Wrong?", Economic & Political Weekly, 28 April.

Molyneux, Maxine, (1994) 'Women's Rights and the International Context: Some reflections on the post-communist states', *Millennium*, 23:2, LSE, London.

Molyneux, Maxine, (2001) Women's Movements in International Perspective: Latin America and Beyond, Palgrave, London.

Moore, Gwen, and Gene Shackman, (1996) 'Gender and Authority: A Cross-National Study', Social Science Quarterly, Vol. 77. Cross-National Study', Social Science Quarterly, Vol. 77.

Moser Caroline O.N. (1993), Gender Planning and Development: Theory, Practice and Training, Routledge, London.

Moser Caroline O.R. (1989), "Gender Planning in the Third World: Meeting Practical and Strategic Needs", World Development, Vol.17, Issue 11, November.

Moser, Caroline & Moser, A. (2006) Gender Mainstreaming Since Beijing: IN Women: Struggle for Existence by Equity Foundation, Patna, Bihar.

Nair, Janaki (1996), Women and Law in Colonial India: A Social History (Delhi: Kali for Women).

Narayan, D. & Petesch, P. (Ed.) (2002) Voices of the Poor from Many Lands, Oxford University Press, New York.

National Alliance of Women (2008), Engendering 11th Five Year Plan: Removing Obstacles, Creating Opportunities, National Alliance of Women, New Delhi.

NCUES (2007), Report on Conditions of Work and Promotion of Livelihoods in the Unorganized Sector, New Delhi, August.

NCUES (2009), The Challenge of Employment in India: An Informal Economy Perspective, Government of India, New Delhi, April.

Nei, R.N. and Verba, S. (1975) "Political Participation". In Fred I. Green Stein and Nelson W. Polsby (eds.). Handbook of Political Science, Vol. 4 Massachusetts: Addisson-Wesly Pub.Co. P 4.

New Age, (2007), Editorial. "Women's Participation in Policy making non-negotiable", September 14.

Nie, N. H., Powell, Jr., G. B. and K. Prewitt, (1969), 'Social Structure and Political Participation: Developmental Relationships', American Political Science Review, 63, 361-78, 808-32.

Nie, N. H., S. Verba and J. Kim, (1974), 'Political Participation and The Life Cycle', Comparative Politics, 6, 319-40.

NIPCCD (2007), Statistics on Women in India, National Institute of Public Cooperation and Child Development, New Delhi.

NIPCCD (2010), "Research Abstracts on Human Development, 1998-2009", Documentation Centre for Women and Children, New Delhi.

Noeleen (2006) Gender Responsive Budgeting and Women's Reproductive Rights, UNIFEM , New York.

Norman D. Palmer (1976), Elections and Political Development: The South Asian Experience, Vikas Publish.ng House, New Delhi.

Norris, (Eds) (1993), Gender and Party Politics, Sage, London.

Norris, Pippa, (1985) 'Women's Legislative Participation in Western Europe', West European Politics, Vol. 18.

Norris, Pippa, (1987) Politics and Sexual Equality, Lynne Rienner, London. Norris, Pippa, (1987), Politics and Sexual Equality, Lynne Rienner, London.

Norris, Pippa, (2000) 'Breaking the Barriers: Positive Discrimination Policies for Women', In J. Klausen and C. S. Maier (eds.), *Has Liberalism Failed Women? Parity, Quotas and Political Representation*, New York: St. Martin's Press.

Norris, Pippa, and Joni Lovenduski, (1995) Political Recruitment: Gender, Race and Class in the British Parliament, Cambridge University Press, Cambridge.

NPC (2005), State Gender Development Report, National Productivity Council, New Delhi.

NSO (2010), Employment and Unemployment Situation in India National Sample Survey Office, Government of India, New Delhi.

Oakes, Ann, and Elizabeth Almquist, (1993) 'Women in National Legislatures: A Cross-National Test of Macrostructural Gender Theories', Population Research Policy and Review, Vol. 12.

Oxfam (2017) Development In Bihar: Some Policy Prescriptions From Gender Lens, Oxfam India, Policy Brief, 24, July, New Delhi

Palmer, D.N. (1976) Election and Political Development: The South Asian Experience. New Delhi. Vikas Pub. House.P 50-57.

Pandey, S.P. & Singh, A.K. (2008), Project Report on Socio-Economic Status of Muslim Women in Uttar Pradesh, G.B. Pant Institute of Studies in Rural Development, Lucknow.

Parker, Andrew (1995), Decentralization: The Way Forward for Rural Development, Policy and Research Working Paper, Washington D.C., World Bank.

Paxton, Pamela, (1997) 'Women in National Legislatures: A Cross-National Analysis', Social Science Research, Vol. 26.

Peterson, V.S. and Runyan, A. (1993), 'Global Gender Issues', USA, Westview Press Inc.

Petras, James (1999), 'Globalization: A Socialist Perspective', EPW, February 20, Mumbai.

Phillips, Anne, (1991) Engendering Democracy, Polity Press, Cambridge.

Pinto, M. (1995), "Development Through Empowerment of Women in India", Kurukshetra, August.

Pittman, J.J. (1996), Working Women, Earth Scan, London & New York.

Planning Commission (2006), Approach Paper to the Eleventh Five Year Plan, Planning Commission, New Delhi.

Planning Commission (2008), Report of the Working Group on Empowerment of Women for the Eleventh Plan, Planning Commission, Govt. of India, New Delhi.

Prasad, D. Ravindra, (2014) *Women Empowerment in Urban Governance in India*, Indian Journal of Public Administration, Vol. LX-3, July-September.

Rajput, Pam (1993), "Women Leadership at the Grassroot Level in Punjab" in Women's Participation in Politics, ed. Susheela Kaushik. New Delhi : Vikas Publishing House.

Rakesh Basant (2012), Education and Employment among Muslims in India: An Analysis Of Patterns And Trends, Indian Institute of Management Ahmedabad-, September.

Raman, Vasanthi. (2002), 'The Implementation of quotas for women: The Indian experience" Quota Report Series, IDEA Publication.

Ramirez, Francisco O., Yasemin Soysal, and Suzanne Shanahan, (1997), 'The Changing Logic of Political citizenship: Cross-National Acquisition of Women's Suffrage Rights, 1890 to 1990', American Sociological Review, Vol. 62.

Randall, Vicky, (1987) Women in Politics, Macmillan, London.

Rao Nitya (1998), "Researching Empowerment: A Grass Roots Women's Perspective", Economic and Political Weekly, Vol.33, No.6.

Ratansi, Y. (2008, June). Report of the Standing Committee on the Status of Women. Towards gender responsive budgeting: rising to the challenge of achieving gender equality. 39th Parliament, 2nd session, p. 20-21.

Ravi, Rohan Sandhu (2014), Women in Party Politics, Brookings Institution India Center, India.

Reynolds, Andrew, (1999) 'Women in African Legislatures and Executives: The Slow Climb to Power, Electoral Institute of South Africa.

Rondinelli, D. (1981), Government Decentralization in Comparative Perspective: Theory and Practice in Developing Countries, International Review of Administrative Science.

Roy, Kalpana (1999), Women in Indian Politics, Rajat Publications, Delhi.

Rule, Wilma, (1981) 'Why Women Don't Run: The critical Contextual Factors in Women's Legislative recruitment', Western political Quarterly, Vol. 34, No. XX.

Rule, Wilma, (1994) 'Women's Underrepresentation in Electoral Systems', Political Science and Politics, Vol. XXVII, No. 4.

Rule, Wilma, and Joseph Zimmerman, (Eds.), (1994) Electoral Systems in Comparative Perspective: Their Impact on Women and Minorities, Greenwood Press.

Rush, M. and Althoff, P., (1971). Introduction to Political Sociology, London: Thomas Nelson.

Rustagi, Pareet, (2004), "Women and Development in South Asia", South Asian Journal, April-June.

Rustagi, Pareet, (2004), "Women and Development in South Asia", South Asian Journal, April-June.

Saiyid, Dushka. (2001), "Women in Politics-Problems of participation: A case study of Pakistan", ISSI Journal, XXI No. 2 Summer.

Sawer, M. (1998), Efficiency, Effectiveness and Equity, IN G. Davis et.al. (Ed), Decentralization by Default : Local Government and The View From Villages in Gambia , Public Administration and Development , Vol.14 , No 3.

Schonfeld, W. R. (1975), 'The Meaning of Democratic Participation', World Politics, 28, 134-58.

Sengupta, A.K. And Singh, A.K. (1988), Empowerment Of Women: An Operational Strategy, MMEM, Business Review, Institute of Development Studies, Lucknow University.

Sengupta, P. (1974), The Story of Women In India, New Delhi: Indian Book Co.

Seshadri, K . (1976) Political Linkages and Rural Development, National Publishing House. New Delhi, p. 175.

Seth, Mira (2001), Generating Awareness, Yojana, August, Vol. 45.

Seth, Mira (2001), Women And Development : The Indian Experience,New Delhi: Sage Publications.

Shiva, V. Staying Alive: Women, Ecology and Development, Zed Books, London.

Singh, A.K. & Singh, A.P. (2012), Care and Protection of Girl Children in India, Bal Vikas Prakashan, New Delhi.

Singh, A.K. (2009), Empowerment of Rural Women through Micro Financing, Serials Publications, New Delhi.

Singh, A.K. (2010), An Overview of Gender Budgeting in India, IN Gender Budgeting and Women Empowerment in India Edited by Singh, A.K. et.al., Serials Publications, New Delhi.

Singh, A.K. (2013), Gender Mainstreaming in Urban Administration, IN Empowerment of Women Through Gender Budgeting Edited by Mita Ashish Shah, Aviskar Publishers, Jaipur.

Singh, A. K. and Kumar, Ravish (2010), Women Empowerment and Development Discourse in India, IN Gender Budgeting and Women Empowerment in India, Edited by Singh, A.K. et.al., Serials Publications, New Delhi.

Singh, A.K. and Singh, A.P. (2012), Care and Protection of Girl Children in India, Rashtriya Bal Vikas Prakashan, New Delhi.

Singh, A.K. and Singh, R.V.P. (2010), Impact of Swa-Shakti and Swayam Siddha Project on Women Empowerment, IN Gender Budgeting and Women Empowerment in India, Edited by Singh, A.K. et.al., Serials Publications, New Delhi.

Singh, A.K. et.al, (Ed.) (2013), Gender Violence in India: Emerging Issues, Challenges and Way Forward, Rashtriya Bal Vikas Prakashan, New Delhi.

Singh, A.K. et.al. (2010), Gender Budgeting and Women Empowerment in India, Serials Publications, New Delhi.

Singh, A.K. et.al. (Ed.) (2012), Women Entrepreneurship in India: Issues, Challenges and Way Forward, Serials Publications, New Delhi.

Singh, A.P. and Singh, A.K. (Ed.) (2013), Care and Protection of Girl Children: Emerging Issues, Challenges and Way Forward, Rashtriya Bal Vikas Prakashan, New Delhi.

Singh, M.K. (2006), Challenges of Globalization on Indian Higher Education, University News, 44 (19), May.

Singh, Purnima et al (2009), "Perceived Justice of Available Opportunities and Self Esteem and Social Exclusion: A Study of Three Religious Groups in India", Psychological Studies,54.

Singh, S. & Srivastava, S.P. (2001), Gender Equality Through Women Empowerment, Bharat Book Centre, Lucknow.

Singh, S.K. & Singh A.K. (2004) OBC Women: Status & Educational Empowerment, New Royal Book Company, Lucknow.

Singh, S.P. (2010), Gender Budgeting: A Tool for Women Empowerment Through SHGs in Jhabua District of M.P. in Gender Budgeting and Women Empowerment in India, Edited by Singh, A.K. et.al., Serials Publications, New Delhi.

Singh, S.P. and Biswas, P.K. (2010), An Overview of Changing Scenario of Women Empowerment in India's Five Year Plans, A Futuristic Vision of 11th Five Year Plan Towards Women's Sustainability in Global Era, in Gender Budgeting and Women Empowerment in India Edited by Singh, A.K. et.al., Serials Publications, New Delhi.

Smith, B. (1985) Decentralization: The Theoretical Dimension of the State, George Allen and Unwind, London.

Southard, Barbara (1993), "Colonial Politics and Women's Rights: Woman Suffrage Campaigns in Bengal, British India in the 1920s", Modem Asian Studies, 27, Printed in Great Britain.

Tedin, Kent L. David W. Brady and Arnold Vedlitz, (1977) "Sex Differences in Political Attitudes and Behaviour: The Case for Situational Factors.

Thomas, Sue, (1994) How Women Legislate, Oxford University Press, New York.

Times of India, (2008), Editorial. "Empowerment of Women", March 09.

U. N. (2002). Demographic Year Book 2000, Department of Economic and Social Affairs, United Nations, New York.

UN Women (2015) Women and Sustainable Goals , UN Women, Nairobi, Kenya.

UNDP (2003) Human Development Report, UNDP, Washington.

UNICEF (2007), Women and Children: The Double Dividend of Gender Equality, UNICEF, New York.

UNIFEM (2013) Locating Gender in the 12th Five Year Plan Approach: Issues Emerging from a Gendered Analysis, UNIFEM, New Delhi.

Unni, J (2010), "Informality and Gender in the Labour Market for Muslims: Has Education been a Route Out of Poverty", in Basant R and Shariff, A (eds.) (2010), Handbook of Muslims in India: Empirical and Policy Perspectives, Oxford University Press.

Vega, Arturo, and Juanita M. Firestone, (1995) 'The Effects of Gender on Congressional Behavior and the Substantive Representation of Women', Legislative Studies Quarterly, Vol. 20.

Verba, S. and Almond, G.A. (1963) Civic Culture : Political Attitudes and Democracy in Five Nations. Princeton: Princeton University Press.

Verba, S. and Nie, N.H. (1972) Participation in America. Harper and Row New York, P. 104-108.

Verba, Sidney (2000) Political Participation and Political Equality, A Seven Nation Comparison , Cambridge: Cambridge University Press, p. 39.

Verba, Sidney Norman H. Nie, (1972) Participation in America: Political Democracy and Social Equality , Harper Row, New York, p. 4.

Verma, R.B.S. and Singh, A.K. (2013), Women Empowerment in India: Perspective, Status and Issues, IN Women Empowerment: Status and Perspective, Edited by Mandot, Manju et.al., Himanshu Publications, Jaipur.

Verma, R. B. S., et. al. (Ed) (2007), The Indian State and Women's Problematic: Running with the Hare and Hunting with the Hounds, Serials Publications, New Delhi.

Visaria, L.(1974). "Demographic transition among Parsis: 1881-1971, Economic and Political Weekly 9 (41).

Visram, Rozina (1992), Women in India and Pakistan: The Struggle for Independence from British Rule (Cambridge University Press).

Vyasulu, P and V Vyasulu (1999), "Women in Panchayati Raj: Grassroots Democracy in India, Experience in Malgudi", Background Paper No. 4, New Delhi, United Nations Development Programme.

Weiner, M. (1966) Political Participation and Political Development", in M. Weiner, (ed.). Modernization, New York: Basic Books.

Weiner, Myron "Political Participation: Crisis of Political Process" in Norman D. Palmer., pp. 57-58.

Weisskoph T E (2010), "Is Positive Discrimination a Good Way to Aid Disadvantaged Communities?" in Basant R and Shariff, A (eds.) (2010), Handbook of Muslims in India: Empirical and Policy Perspectives, Oxford University Press.

Wichterich, C. (Ed.) (2010), In Search of Economic Alternatives for Gender and Social Justice: Voices from India, Heinrich Boll Stiftung – Wide, Brussels, Belgium.

World Bank (2001), Engendering Development: Through Gender Equality in Rights, Resources and Voice, World Bank Policy Research Report, Oxford University Press, Washington.

World Bank (2004), Fiscal Decentralization to Rural Governments in India, World Bank, OUP, New Delhi.

World Bank (2011), Gender Equality and Development, World Bank Report, Washington, D. C.

Yadav, Yogendra (2000), "Understanding the Second Democratic Upsurge" in Francine R Frankel,

Young, K. (2002) WID, GAD and WAD, In Vandana Desai and Robert B. Porrter (Ed). The Companion to Development Studies, Arnold, London.

Index